THE RIVER Severn

A JOURNEY FOLLOWING THE RIVER FROM THE
ESTUARY TO ITS SOURCE

First published in Great Britain
by Hunt End Books 2004

This edition published by Brewin Books Ltd,
Studley, Warwickshire, B80 7LG in 2005
www.brewinbooks.com

Reprinted February 2007

ISBN 10: 1 85858 273 3
ISBN 13: 978 1 85858 273 3

Acknowledgements

The publisher would like to thank those who helped
with the preparation of this book or gave
permission to reproduce illustrations and photographs:
Anne Bradford
Margaret Cooper, Halfshire Books
Caroll Davies
Jim Ralph, Forestry Commission. Wales
Ieuan Rees
Ironbridge Gorge Museum Trust
Local History Department, Gloucester Public Library
The Waterways Trust, National Waterways Museum
Powysland Museum and Montgomery Canal Centre
Brian Standish

Printed in Great Britain by
Cromwell Press Ltd

The cover photograph is of the river Severn at Kempsey
The frontispiece photograph is of the river Severn near Longney
The back cover photograph of a wreck in the estuary was taken at Purton

CONTENTS

THE RIVER Severn

A JOURNEY FOLLOWING THE RIVER FROM THE ESTUARY TO ITS SOURCE

Text, photography and design by
John Bradford

BREWIN BOOKS

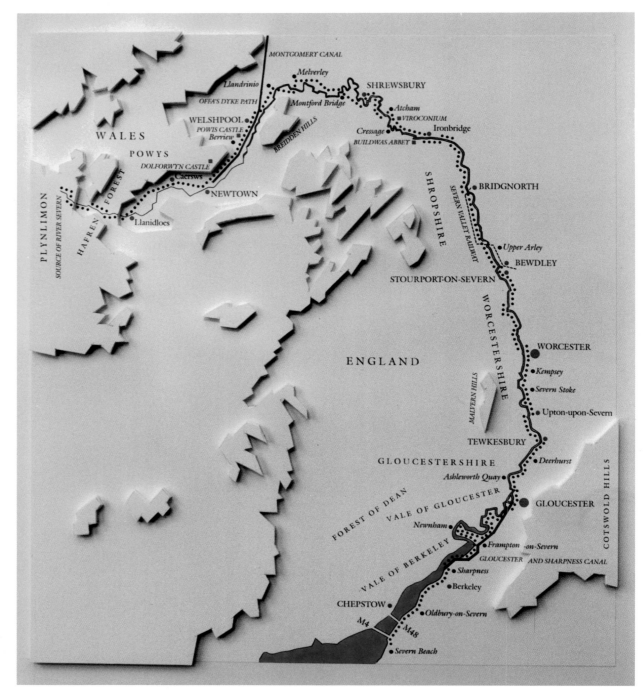

The dotted line on this map represents the route followed along the Severn Way footpath from Severn Beach to Plynlimon.

Introduction

The Severn is the river with the second highest tidal reach in the world, and the Severn Bore, a tidal wave that surges up the narrowing river is a phenomenon that often features in the newspapers in spring and autumn when it is particularly dramatic and makes a good photograph. Otherwise, apart from periodic floods, the river flows through parts of England and Wales that, if not quite backwaters, rarely make the front pages of national newspapers.

This journey follows the Severn from the magnificent new bridge over the estuary at Severn Beach to its source 210 miles away, high on Plynlimon in Wales. At first the vast and empty spaces of the estuary resemble a sea more than a river, but at Gloucester it assumes the character of a slow-flowing high-banked river, and this it retains for much of its length.

Eventually, nearing Newtown it assumes its final form of an upland fast-flowing river with stony beaches, rocks and waterfalls.

The countryside changes in harmony with the river. At first flat, windswept and dominated by the sheer scale of the estuary, it soon mellows into typical Gloucestershire meadows, woods and farms, seen against the background of the Cotswold escarpment to the east and the undulating hills of the Forest of Dean to the west. Rural Worcestershire is followed by Shropshire and the Welsh Marches where the walker becomes aware of hills on the horizon to which the river is leading him. At Newtown, the route, having so far followed closely the river bank, at last departs and takes to the hills before descending to the pretty little town of Llanidloes. From here begins the ascent of Plynlimon to the spring that is the river's source.

During this journey the cathedral cities of Gloucester and Worcester will have been visited, as will Tewkesbury with its beautiful Romanesque abbey.

Bridgnorth and Shrewsbury, two of the most attractive old towns in the country will have been passed through, as have several smaller towns and villages with their vernacular architecture and local history. Ironbridge, cradle of the industrial revolution, now a World Heritage Site, is on the route. But for me it was the very small, secretive places like Ashleworth Quay, the ruins of Buildwas abbey and the two Saxon churches at Deerhurst that had the deepest impact. At these and many others I lingered, soaking up the atmosphere, grateful that the river had revealed its hidden charms as well as its more familiar attractions.

A guiding principle for this book was that I would only feature places visited by the route. The walker cannot, for instance, cross the Severn in order to visit Lydney on the opposite bank, without making a long detour via the nearest bridge. This, however, causes few problems. First, because the route changes from side to side of the river, and secondly, because all of the towns above Gloucester have bridges. I broke the rule a few times, notably for Ashleworth Quay and Shrawley Woods which I thought were too good to miss, so these and one or two other places are found within these pages.

John L Bradford

The common reed has colonised much of the riverside below Gloucester.

Welsh slate being unloaded from a trow at the quay below Llanthony bridge in the early 1920s.
National Waterways Museum.

THE RIVER Severn
GLOUCESTERSHIRE

The estuary and the tideway

Severn Beach to Littleton Pill

A vast landscape composed of sky and sea, reminiscent of a Turner canvas, greeted me as I gazed over the estuary at Aust. A cream-coloured haze on the horizon was all that distinguished the blue sky from the equally blue sea. Slashed horizontally across this picture, narrowing dynamically towards the opposite shore, the bridge carrying the M48 from England to Wales cast a cobalt blue shadow on to the surface of the water and either side of this a million ripples reflected the sun's glare.

Earlier that day I had begun this walk at Severn beach where the new bridge, Britain's longest river crossing, carries the M4 over the estuary. Here, great slabs of concrete the size of small fortresses stride out above the sand, rocks and sea. Three pillars rise from each slab to support, high above, the road along which tiny dots move like ants on a branch. Two more convincing examples of man's technological mastery over nature would be hard to find.

A very different sort of scene awaits the walker who follows the river Severn all the way to its source in mid Wales. Plynlimon, a sprawling, bleak, exposed range of mountains, 2000 feet high, has been little troubled by man's attentions over the last few thousand years, other than having its coarse grasses above the tree line grazed by sheep. It is there that Britain's longest river has its unremarkable beginning - two upright posts and a small patch of soggy mosses and cotton grass. There can be few greater contrasts of scenery in the country than these two extremes, linked by a common theme.

No great flourish marks the beginning of the Severn Way. Nothing to signify a starting point, or at least none that I could find. Just a standard little white plastic disc featuring a graphic of a trow and 'Severn Way' in blue, identical to all the countless other discs along the river's length (although strangely, not below Gloucester). There is a visitor centre and car park, but it is the most neglected-looking place one could wish for.

Having stared in wonder for a while at the Severn Beach bridge I began to walk up river to its companion. In between I gained an early sense of the pleasure to come during the next few days of walking. The path largely follows the top of a floodbank separating the estuary, with its beaches, salt marshes, sea birds, driftwood and high tide debris, from the land which is typical English countryside - hedged fields full of cattle and sheep, small woods and distant farms and villages. One side blue, gold, brown and grey, the other every variety of green.

A sign defaced with graffiti at Littleton Pill advises the public that 'It is unsafe to bathe here due to strong currents and mud'. One look at the chocolate-coloured glutinous mud banks and the trickle of brown water would be sufficient, I thought, to put anyone off. The notice was superfluous. But on second thoughts ...

Littleton Pill to Windbound Inn, Shepperdine

A little flock of nine goldfinches alighted on a patch of thistles ahead of me that were growing on the side of the floodbank. For those who like solitude, this is the place to be. Apart from sea birds - specks on the distant mudflats, and herds of cows grazing the broad wasteland between the fields and the estuary, there was not a soul in sight. The Friesian cows seemed to be attracted to the floodbank, and though most ambled off as I approached, some continued to eat the grass whilst the odd bloody-minded individual stood resolute in her refusal to move out of the way. Avoiding unnecessary confrontations I descended the bank, passed the cow and regained the footpath a few paces further on.

The newest of the Severn bridges, opened in 1996, rests partly on an outcrop of rock called 'English Stones'.

Old Passage, the centuries old river-crossing, was the place chosen for the building of the Severn Bridge which replaced a ferry service when it was opened in 1966. From Aust Rock it spans the estuary to Beachley, then continues over the river Wye to enter Wales near Chepstow.

Evening light over The Pill near New Passage.

The distinctive sound of rigging slapping rhythmically in the wind against the masts of boats confirmed my belief that I was nearing Oldbury Pill. Two dozen or so small craft sat on the mud well above the water line, but there was no sign of human activity. When I returned later in the afternoon some of the boats were floating in the rising tide.

The huge tidal reservoir, excavated in 1992 to provide water for Oldbury Power Station, is as impressive as the twin-reactor nuclear station itself. Unimaginable volumes of water flow up and down the estuary every day. The tide at Chepstow on the opposite bank rises and falls 48 feet.

Windbound Inn, Shepperdine, to Berkeley

At 6pm I was still sitting on the floodbank watching the sun go down over the estuary, at the end of a day that had been exceptionally bright and calm. Barely a ripple disturbed the surface of the water. A flock of seagulls flew low over a pool encircled by rocks, their mirror images reflecting black in its surface. I was reluctant to end such a perfect day, knowing that the Severn estuary is rarely this benign and can look and feel very different when clouds gather and the wind blows along its unprotected shores.

Narrow lanes beside water-filled dykes zig-zag their way from isolated villages inland towards the estuary, where, unable to go any further, they converge on a rough track leading to the Windbound Inn. Tucked in behind the Severn floodbank, this inn was once a favourite haunt of bargees. With their barges safely secured to iron posts, they spent the next three to four days getting drunk. Eventually arriving at their destination, they excused the delay by saying that they had been 'windbound' which is how the inn got its name.

The fields near to the Windbound Inn are full of medieval ridge and furrow stretching down to within a few yards of the floodbank. Nearby are two interesting houses, one formerly a 14th century chapel, the other, which is whitewashed, was the house of a lightkeeper.

Hills Flats, a wide area of flat rocks and sand, have a number of lines of old posts driven into the sand stretching so far out into the estuary that the end of the line is hard to determine. The fishermen who erected these traps must have known the estuary and its treacherous tides very well to have taken such risks. A little further on Hayward Rock becomes a waterfall at low tide, the muted sound of which on a calm day is just audible.

I switched to automatic pilot for the dreary stretch of the route between the nuclear power station and Berkeley.

Berkeley is a small town, famous for its castle. Infamous would perhaps be a better word to use, for it was within the walls of Berkeley castle in 1327 that Edward II was brutally murdered. Thomas Berkeley and his wife Catherine, owners of the castle at that time, were rewarded with a fine family tomb in St Mary's church, he in full armour and both of them with their hands clasped in prayer. A little over a century earlier in 1215 the barons met at the castle before going on to Runnymede to force King John to sign Magna Carta. Events of national importance happen elsewhere these days and castles must make a living as best as they can. My visit coincided with a 'Homes and Gardens' exhibition which was taking place in the field below the castle walls.

The decaying remains of a basket fishery weir. In river parlance these were 'fixed engines made up of kipes, butts and forewheels'. In lay terms, they were lines of stakes driven into the mud to which were attached funnel-shaped woven baskets, or kipes, for trapping salmon. Occasionally, small sharks and sturgeon would end up in the traps. At high tide the weirs were vulnerable to boats straying out of the channels and to flood debris, so repairs were a constant problem.

The light-keeper's house at Shepperdine.

Lydney Sand.

The small yacht club at Oldbury Pill where it is necessary to make a one-and-a-half mile detour via Oldbury village in order to reach the opposite bank a few yards away.

The Norman castle at Berkeley was begun in 1067, rebuilt in 1154 and substantially altered during the 14th century. The manor of Berkeley was given by William the Conqueror to Roger de Berkeley, whose family held it until they chose the losing side during the years of the civil war between King Stephen and Matilda. The confiscated estates then passed to Robert FitzHarding whose descendents have lived there ever since.

Berkeley to Purton

Recent industrial developments at Sharpness Docks, including the creation of new roads, have caused the maps in the guide book to become out-of-date and unreliable. 'Severn Way' signposts helped me to find my way round the changed route, but at one critical junction there was no sign, so hopelessly confused, I ended up at the Port Authority offices seeking help and I was soon back on the route.

From Sharpness, the Severn Way follows the towpath of the Gloucester and Sharpness Canal as far as Frampton-on-Severn, where it resumes its usual course along the river's bank. This is the first of two canal walks encountered on the Severn Way, the other being the Montgomery Canal in Wales. The two are very different, not least in size, the Gloucester and Sharpness Canal being several times wider than the Welsh canal. It is also open to traffic, unlike long sections of the Montgomery Canal. After a hesitant beginning in 1794, Thomas Telford took over responsibility for its construction in 1817 and the work was completed in 1827. At that time the canal was the widest and deepest in the world and enabled large ships to dock at Gloucester without negotiating the hazardous shifting sands of the Severn estuary.

The first mile and a half of the towpath consists of a narrow bank a few yards wide, separating the canal from the river estuary. A railway once crossed the canal here by means of a swing bridge on a circular abutment. A further bridge carried the track on and over the estuary, but it was damaged by two runaway barges and was dismantled in 1960.

Passing the monumental remains of the canal railway bridge, I noticed a pair of Great Crested Grebes. They were in their winter plumage and repeatedly dived under the water, re-emerging a few seconds later, rarely in the spot where I expected them to be. Coming together at one point, the pair touched beaks, engaged in a little head shaking and separated to resume their diving. They are enchanting birds with charming bonding habits, and are lucky to have survived the 18th and 19th century fashion for women's muffs, collars and boas made from their feathers and skins.

A mature hedge hides the view of the estuary from walkers on the towpath near Purton, but it is pierced in places by tunnel-like tracks. Using one of these and expecting to have revealed the by now familiar scene of reed-covered mud banks, sandy beaches and a great expanse of water (which indeed it did) I was nevertheless astonished to be confronted by a graveyard of old trows. These flat-bottomed sailing boats, ideal for use on the tidal Severn, were developed centuries ago in the river's many boatyards. They lay in varying stages of decay partly buried in the reeds and coarse vegetation and were drawn up in parallel formation like beached Viking longboats. At Purton, the trows have been assimilated into the mudbanks, their prows protruding from the low cliffs and pointing towards the sea. A more romantic and melancholy scene it would be hard to invent. The trows were deliberately beached here when the river trade declined, with the intention that they might perform one last service and help to prevent soil erosion by the tides.

Sharpness Docks were opened in 1827. The government of the time gave a loan for the construction on condition that veterans from the Napoleonic war were employed. The docks provided access to Gloucester from the sea for vessels of up to 750 tons along the Glouces-ter and Sharpness canal. The docks today are still a busy port, capable of handling vessels of 7,000 tons.

The rotting timbers of redundant trows, beached near Purton, in the hope of reducing erosion along the banks of the estuary.
It is estimated that over 2,000 trows were built in boatyards and on the banks of the Severn during the five centuries of their use, before the arrival of the railways in the 19th century led to their decline.

Trows were to the river Severn in the past, what HGVs are to our motorways. Flat-bottomed and with masts that could be lowered for passing under bridges, trows were capable of sailing up the narrowest of creeks with the tide, sitting on the mud at low water and loading or unloading cargo, then sailing away on the next high tide.

Varying considerably in size from 90 tons or more to much smaller vessels, they were ideally suited to conditions on the Severn and the estuary, as well as other rivers in the west of England and South Wales. Originally having square sails, later trows were fore and aft rigged, an improvement for catching the wind.

The sun sets behind a wrecked trow near Purton, and below, the first of several swing bridges allowing vehicles to cross the Gloucester and Sharpness canal.

Purton to Frampton-on-Severn

Two days had elapsed since my previous outing, which was sufficient time for the pair of grebes I saw then to catch up with me. They were now a mile or so above Purton. Unless, of course, these were another pair of grebes. There are many coots and moorhens on the canal, the coots in particular being prone to making noisy dashes on the approach of walkers, across the surface of the water to the opposite bank with a great deal of splashing. A lonely female tufted duck and a kingfisher also put in an appearance. Surprisingly, the kingfisher proved to be the only one I saw on the entire walk along the river Severn.

Five swing bridges are encountered between Purton and Frampton-on-Severn, each with a bridge-keeper's cottage which are all built to a similar classical design featuring fluted Doric columns. I personally think they look rather comic like garden sheds with grand entrances. The two bridges at Purton appear to be remote-controlled but the others rely on muscle power. It being a Saturday, and a sunny one too, the towpath was quite busy with walkers, fishermen and cyclists, as was the canal with boats and barges, so I didn't envy the bridge-keepers their jobs. They were constantly engaged in winding antique-looking rusty winches that took on a life of their own, spinning furiously once the bridge was in motion.

The bridge at Shepherds Patch provides access for visitors to the famous Slimbridge Wildfowl and Wetland Trust which lies midway between the canal and the estuary.

Crossing Splat Bridge at Frampton-on-Severn, I took the precaution of enquiring what time the bridge closed and whether it was left in a position to benefit road or river traffic. 'Five-thirty pm and road traffic' was the answer, so I was reassured that I was in no danger of becoming stranded on the wrong side of the canal.

Frampton-on-Severn to Arlingham

A notice on Fretherne bridge makes the claim that Frampton-on-Severn has the longest village green in England. Rosamund's Green, named after Jane Clifford, Henry II's mistress, is certainly both long and wide. Jane Clifford, nicknamed Rosamund (rose of the world) by Henry, is said to have been born at Manor Farm, which overlooks the green. Two of her relatives are buried in Saint Mary's church, their effigies lying end-to-end in separate recesses within a wall. As the family's fortunes improved, so too did their living accommodation. A great Palladian mansion, Frampton Court, was built in 1733. The front of the house looks out across a great park, but the back keeps an eye on the village green, albeit from behind the privacy of a high wall and the shelter of ornamental trees.

Most of the village houses are strung out in a line bordering the opposite western side of the green, behind a sequence of three reed-fringed duck ponds. A few rather shabby half-timbered houses near to Frampton Court's entrance gate reminded me of old paintings and early photographs of agricultural workers' hovels, and left me wondering if this was a relic of the days of 'the rich man in his castle, the poor man at his gate'. A few tables placed outside pubs on the edge of the green were occupied by visitors in shorts, lazily enjoying an unseasonably warm autumn afternoon with drinks and cups of coffee.

The distance between Frampton and Framilode is about a mile - twenty minutes or so of walking, whereas to follow the great loop that the river takes between these two points adds something like an extra five hours to the journey. But I was not in a race and not tempted.

The long road down the middle of Frampton-on-Severn's village green ends at a wayside cross on a much smaller green beside Saint Mary's Church. It may be hard to believe, but before the building nearby of the Gloucester and Sharpness canal, a tidal creek brought vessels from the river to within yards of the church.

Pleasure craft on the Gloucester and Sharpness canal near to Splat Bridge, Frampton-on-Severn.

Splat Bridge at Frampton-on-Severn, swings open allowing a barge to pass by. The tower of Saint Mary's church and a bridge-keeper's house are on the right of the picture.

Saul Junction. The Stroudwater Navigation, a canal opened in 1779, connecting the River Severn to Stroud in the Cotswolds, here crosses the Gloucester and Sharpness ship canal in much the same way as a modern cross roads.

Long Wood and Smith's Wood on Hock Cliff look innocent enough, but on reaching the boundary of the latter I found myself on the very edge of the cliff looking at a stile that was clearly ready to disappear over the precipice and into the estuary, its left side post having already done so. Floundering around for a while in the tangle of brambles and ivy, I searched for an alternative exit from the barbed-wire enclosed wood. After taking a second look at the stile I decided that mutilation was a better option than suicide and with great care straddled the barbed wire. Fortunately I am tall.

A little further on an official-looking notice nailed to a post, together with a map, carried the information that the section of the path I had just walked was closed due to a landslide and offered an alternative route.

The area enclosed by the loop of the river has an indefinable air of detachment. It is, after all, close to being an island and contact with the mainland across the river by boat is probably less frequent now than at any time in the past. The bell in Arlingham church tolls the hours but there is little sign of activity outside in the lane. A much-patched wall, opposite, looks as though it is crumbling away, the brickwork having lost most of its mortar.

There are a wide variety of houses ranging from the rather grand to the frankly scruffy, indicating a population that, unlike much of the rest of the country, is not yet segregated according to income and class.

Arlingham to Priding

Many of the older houses in this bit of Gloucestershire are built with a distinctive brick, presumably local, which varies in colour from pale pink to pale yellow and grey. Together they make a pleasingly mellow mosaic of warm colours.

The lane beside Arlingham church leads directly to the river bank where I discovered that overnight a very high tide had left all the land between the floodbank and the river under shallow pools of water. Further on, near Priding, where the path briefly enters a small wood, the tide had left a film of brown mud on which it was only with difficulty that I managed to remain upright.

Between Arlingham and Priding the route stays on top of the floodbank, but all the visual interest lies along the water's edge on the opposite side of the river. Bullo Pill was for many years a coal port handling up to 20,000 tons of coal from the Forest of Dean annually. It had both wharves and locks.

Newnham is quite picturesque. Its church stands at the highest point of a cliff that hangs over the river, whilst colour-washed houses descend in steps down to the water's edge. This was for centuries an important crossing point for Welsh drovers taking cattle to London, and a ferry is known to have operated between Newnham and Arlingham as early as 1238 when the king granted an oak tree to a ferrywoman for the purpose of building a boat.

Slightly downstream from the town three or four old ships have come to rest, ending their days quietly rusting and rotting away into the estuary. Between Newnham and Broadoak the water front has a number of attractive and even elegant houses, seen against a background of green fields rising to the soft curve of May Hill.

The Noose, viewed from Hock Cliff. On a calm and sunny day this is as perfect a place to be as any along the 210 miles of the river.

Hock Cliff, left, where fossils may be found in the sedimentary layers.

An intercity train speeds along the west bank of the river Severn near Newnham. Between Gloucester and Cardiff the line never strays far from the river and its estuary.

More wrecked and decaying boats, this time lined up on the far side of the river at Newnham.

A wartime pillbox beside the Severn Way floodbank probably never fired a shot in anger. This was no doubt good news for any soldiers who might have found themselves all alone inside it and utterly exposed to the firepower of an enemy, should one decide to invade England up the Severn estuary.

More beached and decaying old boats can be seen at Strand beside a riverside house, beyond which Garden Cliff, a smooth-faced, layered, fossil-bearing cliff rises almost vertically from the water's edge.

Priding to Elmore Back

The sky turned white with countless seagulls when, for no apparent reason, the entire flock rose from the exposed sandbanks at Priding. There must have been many thousands of them, certainly more than I have ever seen before in one place.

Beyond Longney there is no longer any ambiguity about the Severn's status as river or estuary. From here on it is definitely a river - an exceptionally wide one by British standards, but clearly a river.

This part of the county used to be covered in orchards. A few can still be found but most have been grubbed up to be replaced by fields full of cattle or sheep or crops. However, the remains of old orchards are everywhere. Ancient gnarled trees, heavily laden with apples or pears that ripen and then fall to the ground, are surrounded by rotting yellow fruit. Meanwhile, supermarkets tempt us with fruit from all corners of the globe. Sackfulls of large ripe red apples could be picked from three trees hanging over the riverside path near Wicksgreen.

Flowers are few and far between in October, so a conspicuous splash of yellow caught my attention. It was a clump of Tansy, very healthy-looking and in full bloom a whole month later than it should be according to my reference book. From the fifteenth to the nineteenth century a 'tansye' was an omelette or pancake flavoured with bitter herbs.

Just as Indian Balsam has invaded many stretches of the river bank further up river in Worcestershire and Shropshire, so the common reed has colonised most parts of the river's margins below Gloucester. In recent times reed beds have been planted as water filters, their root systems acting as filters of toxic substances such as heavy metals and nitrates, so perhaps these reeds beside the Severn are performing the same environmentally-friendly service and helping to save the planet. They certainly look as though they are intent on capturing it.

Elmore Back to Gloucester

I could find no symbols for a church on the OS map of Elmore, but I knew the village had one. This, I discovered, is because the parish church is at Bridgemacote, on the road to Longney. Although a little off the Severn Way route, Elmore church is worth the detour to see the exceptionally good table tombs in the churchyard. Carved in high relief on elaborately-shaped tombs, skulls, reapers, corpses and many other death-associated motifs are as skilfully executed as any to be found in Gloucestershire, a county noted for this tradition.

Entertainment on this, not the most attractive part of the route, was provided by wildlife and farm animals. A surf-boarding seagull, riding the fastest part of the Severn's current on a plank of wood sped past me near Minsterworth. At Rea, a metal-barred swing gate within a semi-circular enclosure provides access to the river bank from a footbridge and lane. As I

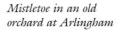
Mistletoe in an old orchard at Arlingham

Broadoak village on the western bank of the Severn.

Newnham, on a cliff above the Severn. Quiet now, it was formerly a prosperous town and has a number of fine houses. In 1764 an enterprising direct service to London by sea was introduced which flourished for a couple of decades before competition from the canals put an end to the service.

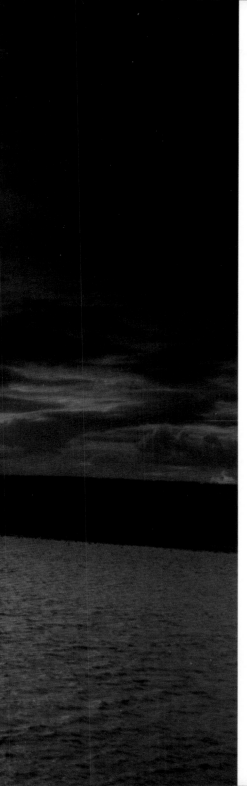

Sunset over the river,
seen from the Anchor
Inn, Epney.

approached, a large white Shire horse standing near the gate edged forward, planting both of his huge feet and the bulk of his body within the enclosure of the gate, from where he looked down on me, his head nodding gently as he sniffed and exhaled air and sized me up. Luckily this was as far as I planned to go that day so a confrontation with this equine bouncer was avoided.

The most amusing sight of the day was at Elmore. A herd of Friesian cows, excited by the presence of a farmer in the field, after dashing to and fro arrived at a low single wire fence, erected to protect some bales of hay. Sitting on the opposite side of the wire was a black and white cat. The cows crowded round the cat, heads lowered, mooing and snorting their annoyance at finding her in their field. For some time the cat ignored the cows but as more arrived and the racket grew in volume she began to show some signs of nervousness.

At Stonebench a permanent house has been created on a large barge (really more like a small ship) that has been beached halfway up the river's bank. A sort of marine conservatory now graces its decks and a line of washing waved gaily in the wind beside her bows.

At Rea a boat has been beached high above the river in a field. Nettles, thistles and wild flowers creep up its bows where water once lapped.

The few miles down river from Gloucester are among the least memorable of this route, consisting largely of a walk beside a giant landfill site, so big that the huge earth-movers in the distance, with their attendant flocks of seagulls, were mere specks on the horizon. At intervals, beside the footpath, sinister-looking bits of high tech equipment were recording the after-life of the refuse deep below my feet.

The route passes the ruins of Llanthony Priory, founded in 1136 by monks fleeing from the priory of the same name in the Black Mountains in Wales, which had been captured by Welsh rebels. The church and cloister was destroyed during the civil war. It presents a rather incongruous spectacle today, surrounded as it is, by industrial buildings and warehouses.

Tansy, growing beside the river.

Distant May Hill, glimpsed between trees, on a bend of the Severn near Wicksgreen. The 971 feet high dome and its crown of trees is a familiar landmark in the Gloucestershire landscape and is easily recognised from many viewpoints in the region.

Apples, hanging over the river bank near Wicksgreen,

High and dry in a field beside the river at Rea, the 'Severn Voyager' was formerly in service with the Severn and Canal Carrying Company. It is now privately owned.

Repiling in progress near to Elmore Back. Interlocking metal plates are pile-driven into the river bed in order to shore up the banks and prevent erosion.

Elmore Court, built by the Lord of the Manor, John Guise, as a home for his bride Jane Pauncefoote. She must have been a patient woman - building work began in 1564 and was finished 24 years later.

Elmore churchyard is notable for its fine collection of table tombs. Within the church are many Guise memorials including one to Johannes and Alicia Gyse of 1472 and one to Sir John Guise, who died in 1895 and was awarded the Victoria Cross for his bravery at the Second Relief of Lucknow.

Gloucester

Nervia Glavenis, modern Gloucester, was a military base established by the Romans in 40-50 AD. The site chosen was the lowest point for a practical crossing of the river Severn. By 96-98 AD Glevum, as it was popularly called, had prospered and expanded and was granted the title of Colonia - the highest status a Roman provincial town could attain. Since the early 1970s archaeological excavations have revealed the Roman North and East Gates, the Forum and Basilica and several private houses that afforded a luxurious lifestyle equal to anywhere in Britain.

Following the departing Romans in the fifth century, the invading Anglo-Saxons settled in Gloucestershire, and in 679 Osric, their king, founded a monastery at Gloucester on or near the site of the present cathedral. William the Conqueror continued the practice of his Saxon predecessors of holding meetings of the Great Council at Gloucester and at one such gathering in 1085 he called for a detailed survey of his new kingdom which resulted in the Doomsday Book.

In 1216 the nine-year-old Henry III was led from the Royal Palace at Kingsholm to his coronation in Saint Peter's Abbey. He is the only English monarch since the Conquest to be crowned outside Westminster. He was a deeply religious man who was responsible for the building of the town's Dominican, Franciscan and Carmelite friaries. The fortunes of medieval Gloucester were strengthened in 1327 when Abbot Thokey accepted for burial at Saint Peter's Abbey the body of Edward II who was murdered at nearby Berkeley Castle. Craftsmen began restoring and beautifying the church and by the 1470s the building had reached its present size. By 1540 the dissolution of the larger monastic houses was well advanced and the episcopal see of Gloucester was established and the abbey church became the Cathedral.

Gloucester's unique asset was its situation at the lowest point on the river Severn where it was possible to build a bridge. The earliest was in use in the twelfth century. There were two bridges in 1226 and later Leland described a succession of three bridges, beginning with a seven-arched stone one near the town, then a fine arched bridge, and finally a quarter-of-a-mile long stone causeway leading to a bridge with eight arches.

There are a number of well-preserved medieval and Tudor houses in Gloucester. In Northgate Street, New Inn dates from about 1450 and was used by pilgrims. It has a galleried courtyard. In Westgate Street, behind the shop front of number 26, through a very narrow passage, is the four-storied timber-framed Judge's house. This was the town house of the Guise and Clifford families. It was also the headquarters of Colonel Massey who was in charge of the city's defence during the Civil War siege of 1643. With only 1500 men he successfully resisted 30,000 Royalists bombarding the town with artillery for 26 days.

Bishop Hooper's Lodging, now the Folk Museum, is the house where the martyr spent his last night before he was burned at the stake by Catholic Queen Mary. The old Berkeley family town house, now the Old Bell Inn, is in Southgate Street.

Gloucester is a city that has not lacked for 'characters'. The cathedral organist, Stephen Jeffries, played 'Lillibulero' as a voluntary at the end of a service celebrating the accession of William of Orange, which scandalised the congregation when 'young gentlwomen invited one another to dance'. 'It were better that the Organs were pulled downe than that they

Gloucester Cathedral and College Green. The tower, begun in 1450 and completed a decade later, is 225 feet high. One of its peal of 12 bells, 'Great Peter', weighs nearly 3 tons and is England's only surviving medieval Bourbon bell. The Norman arcading in the nave has massive columns 32 feet high and 7 feet in diameter. The east window is the largest in England and was installed in 1339 as a memorial to local knights and barons who took part in the Battle of Crecy and the Siege of Calais. Wooden choir stalls dating from 1350 contain 58 misericord seats, decorated with scenes from medieval life. Notable among many memorial tombs in the Cathedral are those of Robert, Duke of Normandy, eldest son of William the Conqueror, and Edward II. The former's tomb is made of painted oak, whilst the murdered King Edward's effigy is of carved alabaster, and is possibly a likeness made soon after his death. Fan tracery in the Great Cloister is the earliest example of this architectural style in the country.

should be so used', they complained, and went on to demand that such an insolent and profane person should be immediately turned out of the church. Jeffries, however, kept his job.

Jemmy Wood, a banker who died in 1836 at the age of 80, was immensely wealthy but notoriously mean. One of his servants attempted to commit suicide by drinking from a bottle marked 'poison'. His life was spared owing to the fact that this was how Jemmy Wood hid his brandy.

When Celia Fiennes was in Gloucester, she found a flourishing riverside port and saw coal from Warwickshire being unloaded from trows onto sledges which were then dragged through the city streets. However, the silting up of the old riverside quay led to plans to construct a canal between Gloucester and the sea. The Gloucester and Sharpness canal was opened in 1827. Gloucester Docks were a transhipment point. Sea-going ships of up to 800 tons docked here, while river craft continued up the Severn to Worcester and beyond. In the 1820s huge brick warehouses were built. These have now been converted for modern uses, including the National Waterways Museum, the Museum of Advertising and Packaging, the Gloucester Antique Centre, offices and restaurants. Dwarfed by these great buildings is the little Mariner's church.

Gloucester's other canal to the river Wye at Hereford was begun with high hopes of success in 1798 but took 47 years to complete and was opened just as the railways arrived, rendering it obsolete.

Infirmary Arches, part of the 13th century south arcade of the monastic infirmary.

This monument to the protestant martyr, Bishop Hooper, marks the place of his execution by fire in 1555. Behind it can be seen the 13th century St Mary's gate which gave access to the abbey precincts.

The Parliament Room, where Richard II held parliament in 1378.

Clock in Southgate Street. Figures representing Ireland, England, Scotland and Wales sound the chimes, leaving the hours to Father Time.

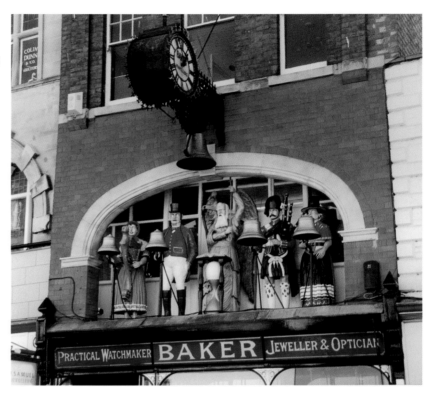

Built by Saint Peter's Abbey, between 1430 and 1450, the New Inn satisfied a need for accommodation for the growing numbers of visitors and pilgrims. Believed in its day to be the largest inn in the country, it was capable of giving hospitality to over 200 people at a time. It is said to be the best example of a medieval galleried inn in Britain. New uses were found for the galleries as times changed. In the 18th century travelling shows - one featuring a two feet ten inch tall Corsiscan Fairy, and a mermaid from the Mexican coast - were offered to the public. Shakespeare's plays are performed here from time to time as are other entertainments.

Busy Southgate Street.

The Main Basin of Gloucester Docks was dug by men using shovels and wheelbarrows between 1794 and 1797. It is 16 feet deep. An impressive group of warehouses beside the basins were built to handle the huge quantities of grain arriving by sea from Ireland, the Mediterranean, the Black Sea and Northern Europe.

Gloucester to Deerhurst

On a sunny autumn day I climbed to the top of Sandhurst Hill, a modest little hill but one with views better by far than many a mountain I have climbed. To the north lies Bredon Hill, east is Gloucester with its cathedral, easily identified, and beyond it the Cotswold escarpment. South is the unmistakable May Hill, and west, behind rolling green fields, the long blue silhouette of the Malvern Hills. In the foreground the river Severn, once a great highway for trade and invaders, now winds quietly past ancient Ashleworth Quay and its Saxon church, fifteenth century court and tithe barn, farm, and diminutive quayside inn. This was once an important river crossing, but it is many years since the ferry boat made its last journey.

'No elver fishing' signs are commonly encountered along the lower reaches of the river Severn. It was not until 1778 that fishing for baby eels was permitted, and only then for personal consumption and not to sell. Every year billions of the young fish, about three inches long, having floated in the Atlantic Ocean currents from their spawning grounds in the distant Sargasso sea, swim up Britain's rivers, eventually to grow to maturity. Anything between twelve and sixty inches in length they then start the long journey back to start the cycle all over again. Unlike other fish, eels are capable of living out of water for short periods of time and therefore sometimes move overland between rivers and lakes. Elvers today are a jealously guarded catch that fetch high prices in foreign markets.

Coombe Hill canal was built in 1796-97 but was never very successful, due to it being subject to repeated flooding, and was abandoned in 1876. It is now a nature reserve looked after by the Gloucestershire Wildlife Trust.

The path passes through an enclosed area of uncultivated land near Apperley. It is a bit of a tangled jungle to walk through but worth the reward of seeing so many wild flowers. Most conspicuous are the violet-blue blooms of Meadow Cranesbill but equally eye-catching are some jumbo-sized clumps of Tufted Vetch, smothered in blooms and looking like large, round, blue cushions.

During the floods of 1958 a 200-ton tanker barge collided with the three-arched cast-iron bridge at Haw Bridge, bringing it down and killing the master of the vessel. The present bridge was built in 1961.

A dark green E-type Jaguar parked next to my VW Polo behind Haw Bridge Inn attracted my attention. I was standing admiring it when a voice behind me said, 'Lovely car, isn't it?' (pause) ... 'I always drove Aston Martins myself'. I was at a loss what to reply to this. My ownership of a long sequence of bottom-of-the-range minis, Renaults, Fiats, Citroens and VWs somehow didn't seem to add up to a fitting response.

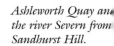

Ashleworth Church. Roods were removed by law in 1548 during the reign of Protestant Edward VI and were replaced by the Royal Coat of Arms. Catholic Mary took these down and Elizabeth I put them back up again. For this reason it is uncertain whether this undoubtedly Tudor coat of arms in Ashleworth Church is that of Edward or his sister Elizabeth. During Victorian times, heraldry of this sort fell out of fashion and was removed but was put back up again in 1988, where it awaits the next change in its fortunes.

Ashleworth Quay and the river Severn from Sandhurst Hill.

Window inserted into the semi-circular doorway of the Saxon church.

The Boat Inn at Ashleworth Quay is on the site of the former ferry. This was the point at which the river towpath changed sides, hence the need for a ferry.

Ashleworth Tithe Barn, near to the church, was erected between 1481 and 1515. It is 120 feet long with 10 bays and has a stone-tiled roof. Belonging to the National Trust, it is open to visitors between March and October.

Haw Bridge Inn.

The Malvern Hills from Sandhurst Hill.

Deerhurst

Deerhurst (the place in the 'wood of the deer') is two miles south of Tewkesbury, beside the river Severn. Two of the best preserved Anglo Saxon churches in England are to be found there only a short distance apart. The Priory Church of Saint Mary dates from 804, although parts of it are thought to be earlier, probably seventh century. High up on a wall at the back of the church, where an apse once stood, is a badly weathered carving of an angel from the eighth century. She now gazes past the ground plan of the missing apse to a farmyard. The church contains two fine animatedly-carved Saxon sculptures of the heads of beasts, as well as a virgin and child in low relief that was originally painted, and a splendid ninth century font. The church was much altered in early times, and once had an upper floor, evidence for which is clearly visible in a blocked-up doorway. Two striking triangular-headed lights in the same wall open into the tower. The Priory House, attached to the church, once formed one side of the monastery's cloisters.

A monk at Deerhurst in the tenth century, Saint Alphege, later became bishop of Winchester and then Archbishop of Canterbury. In 1011 a Danish army besieged Canterbury and captured Alphege and others, demanding ransom for their release. Alphege forbade his people to buy his freedom, which so angered the Danes that in a fit of drunken rage they battered him to death with ox bones.

Later in 1016 the Saxon King Edmund met the Viking King Canute on an island in the river, near to Deerhurst, to agree a treaty partitioning England between them. Edmund ruled Wessex and Canute ruled the north. Within a month Edmund was dead, possibly murdered, and England became part of a Scandinavian empire for the next 25 years.

Odda's chapel, nearby, was rediscovered in 1885 after many years in use, first as a barn and later as a house. In 1675 a dedication stone was dug up in a local orchard. The inscription reads 'Earl Odda had this royal hall built and dedicated in honour of the Holy Trinity for the soul of his brother Aelfric which left the body in this place. Bishop Ealdred dedicated it the second of the Ides of April in the fourteenth year of the reign of Edward King of the English (12th April 1056).

Odda's Chapel, after years of use as a barn and a house, was rediscovered in 1885. It is now in the care of English Heritage.

Deerhurst Church. A blocked doorway in the far corner led to the former cloister, now a private house behind its garden.

The quintessential river Severn in its heartland. Cows graze or rest on high banks near Deerhurst.

Triangular-headed lights opening into the tower of the three-storey Saxon church at Deerhurst. Note also the blocked door at the first floor level of this unique three-storey church.

The weir on the Severn at Tewkesbury.

Tewkesbury

The river Avon flows into the Severn a quarter of a mile or so west of Tewkesbury. A branch of the Avon, called the Mill Avon, which was probably cut by monks in the 12th century to power the abbey mill, passes behind the buildings lining two of the town's main streets, and joins the Severn at Lower Lode half a mile south of the town. A water-powered mill is known to have been in use in 1291 but the present mill dates from 1793 and now serves as a restaurant.

Riverside inn at Lower Lode.

Tewkesbury is a pretty, bustling, slightly dishevelled-looking town constricted in size by the two rivers on one side and low-lying water meadows prone to flooding on the other. Consequently it has never expanded from its original Y-shaped medieval street plan. Modern industrial developments are sited at Ashchurch and Northway to the east of the town. Tewkesbury is one of the country's most complete medieval townscapes with a wealth of good timbered buildings. Some of these are inns, notably the Bell Hotel in Church Street and the Royal Hop Pole Hotel, where Charles Dickens' Mr Pickwick and his companions drank bottled ale, Madeira and port before resuming their journey. In the High Street the Tudor House Hotel was built in 1540 and the Old Black Bear dates from 1308. A very fine row of timber-framed houses in Church Street have been carefully renovated and are now museums.

The Tewkesbury Mop fair, a yearly event in October, dates from the 11th century.

Many narrow alleyways lead off the main streets, the most interesting being Old Baptists Chapel Court which leads to the oldest Baptist chapel in Southern England. This was created in 1623 when existing buildings were converted for use as a place of worship and contains a baptistry used for baptism by total immersion.

At the opposite end of the religious spectrum is the town's principle glory, Tewkesbury Abbey. It is one of the country's most beautiful Romanesque churches, with massive Norman columns in the nave and a 65 feet high recessed arch containing a west window from 1686. Founded in the last decade of the 11th century on the site of a Saxon abbey of 715, the Benedictine Abbey was the last monastery to be dissolved by Henry VIII. Thanks to the generosity of the townspeople of the time who bought it for £453, the Abbey Church is still with us today.

In May 1471 the battle of Tewkesbury raged round the foot of the abbey and proved to be the climax of the Wars of the Roses. 6,000 Lancastrians faced 5,000 Yorkists. Edward IV won the day and the most dangerous of his captive foes were dragged from the abbey where they had sought sanctuary, and tried and executed in the town within days of the battle.

The Mill Avon, Ab Mill, and the tower Tewkesbury Abbey.

West front of Tewkesbury Abbey and the Abbot's Lodging. The recessed Norman arch, 65 feet high, contains a window from 1686 and the Norman choir and transepts are probably Europe's earliest four-storied buildings, completed in the late 12th century. The abbey's Romanesque tower is the largest and best in England, its upper stages displaying graceful interlaced arches. 14 massive columns in the nave, each 30 feet high and over 6 feet in diameter support Romanesque arches. The south ambulatory contains tombs of some of the earlier abbots, including that of Abbot Allen who died in 1202. He wrote a contemporary account of the martyrdom of Saint Thomas Beckett. The de Clares, Dispensers and Beachamps, all noble families, extended and rebuilt the abbey and many of them were buried within its sacred walls, as are the Duke of Clarence and his wife. An organ, originally made for Magdalen College, Oxford, known as the Milton organ, came to Tewkesbury in 1737, after spending some time at Hampton Court Palace during the Commonwealth. The assumption is that it was played at Oxford by the poet and so acquired his name.

Traffic moves slowly along the crowded medieval roads through Tewkesbury.

Tewkesbury is noted for its many narrow alleyways leading off the main streets. This one, Old Baptist Chapel Court, leads to southern England's earliest Baptist chapel.

49

A riverside shrub transformed by frost at Upper Arley.

*Passengers from Stourport-on-Severn arriving at Holt Fleet Hotel
on a steamer in 1905.* Brian Standish

THE RIVER **Severn**

WORCESTERSHIRE

The river's sedate progress through city, town and country

Tewkesbury to Upton-on Severn

Place names can be both revealing or deceptive. Rhydd, a Welsh word meaning a ford, indicates that Welsh drovers probably crossed the river Severn at the place so named, a few miles up river from Upton-on-Severn. Saxons Lode, on the other hand, has nothing to do with Saxons, it being a corruption of Sexton's Lode.

Upton-on-Severn, for centuries, was the only place between Worcester and Gloucester with a bridge over the Severn. By 1599 an old timber bridge was so decayed that it was replaced by a stone one. This, in turn, partly due to arguments about who should pay for its upkeep, fell into disrepair and had to be replaced twice before the present bridge was built in 1939. Upton's prosperity grew with the river trade, peaking in the second half of the eighteenth century, after which, due to the coming of the railways and consequent loss of river-born traffic, it reverted to a small town serving the needs of the local agricultural community. One of the town's inns, the White Lion, achieved literary fame as the location of an episode in Fielding's novel, 'Tom Jones'.

Tewkesbury to Upton-on Severn

The Great Flood of autumn 2000 presented me with an opportunity to photograph some quite spectacular scenery in the Severn Valley below Worcester. Standing on Timberdine bridge, the floods appeared to stretch all the way to the Malvern Hills, whilst further down river at Severn Stoke, the church and pub seemed to be floating on a mirror reflecting the angry black clouds massed above. A man in a small boat was ferrying people to and from their homes and the pub, along a narrow hedge-lined lane, to the partially flooded main road.

Flooding has always been a problem on the Severn. Hollinshead described the great flood of 1484: 'Several persons were drowned in their beds, children in cradles swam about in fields, and beasts were drowned, even on the hills'. In the flood of 1606 an eyewitness says, '... huge and mighty hills of water were seen ... and many hundreds of men, women and children perished ... Many who were rich in the morning were beggars before noon.'.

Kempsey is one of Worcestershire's oldest villages, taking its name from Kemeys, a Saxon chief in 799. There was a monastery in Kempsey at that time and later a church. A country palace was built in fields west of the church to which bishops of Worcester and their retinues were rowed from the cathedral in order to entertain kings and queens with their courts. The palace fell into ruins and by Tudor times had completely disappeared.

Simon de Montfort and his prisoner, Henry III, heard mass in Kempsey church on the morning before the battle of Evesham and would have kneeled near the medieval five-light stained glass windows which are today its greatest treasure.

Approaching Worcester, the Severn Way passes Diglis Lock and the canal basin. The canal links Worcester with Gas Street Basin in Birmingham.

Cool classical Georgian outside but full of medieval timbers inside, the White Lion Hotel's origins go back to the early 1500s. The cobbled car park was once part of a cattle market. Sarah Siddons (1755-1831), the famous actress, performed in a barn at the back of the inn, but its main claim to fame is as the setting for the climactic events of Fielding's novel 'Tom Jones'.

As at Bewdley further up the river, rich merchants in Upton-on-Severn built their houses on the waterfront. The medieval church tower, crowned with an Adam-style cupola, is known locally as 'The Pepperpot'.

The building was ruined during a civil war skirmish but was rebuilt in the 18th century. However, following the collapse of the roof of the church, the whole building was demolished leaving only the tower standing.

Two house owners who bravely opted for something brighter than the town's ubiquitous half-timbered black and white and Georgian brick restraint.

On today's menu at Ye Olde Anchor Inn, 'Beef in Ale Pie'.

Saint Mary's church at Kempsey is built on an Iron Age earthworks that was subsequently used by the Romans. A stone inscribed to the Emperor Constantine was dug up here. A big church in 1200, it was further enlarged between 1250 and 1260 by the addition of a huge chancel with a fine east window and five lancet lights. For 60 years a chestnut tree grew inside the church from a gap behind the tomb of Sir Edmund Wylde. The chestnut from which it grew had been snatched from the hands of a boy during a service by the parish clerk who threw it carelessly away.

13th century glass in the chancel of the church at Kempsey. This figure is believed to be a representation of King Edward the Confessor.

This photograph of stained glass in Kempsey Church originally appeared in 'Worcestershire, A portrait of the county', published by Halfshire Books.

A ford with a bridge for pedestrians at Kempsey.

Severn Stoke transformed by floods in 2000.

Worcester

For those unfamiliar with Worcester, their introduction to the city along the river bank may be something of a surprise. Both sides of the river are green and leafy, right up to the old Watergate, the walls of which record the many flood levels from the past. A passenger ferry still operates from here in summer to the meadows on the opposite side of the river. Steps from Watergate lead directly to College Green which is enclosed by the Cathedral, the King's School buildings, the Deanery, the Old Palace, the 13th century Edgar Tower that once provided access to a long-vanished castle, and the ruins of the Guesten Hall. The timber roof of the Guesten Hall, erected in 1326, is one of the finest in the county, and although no longer in its original setting has fortunately been preserved and can be seen at the Avoncroft Museum of Buildings near Bromsgrove.

Worcester has a long history. Its see was founded in 679 and included Warwickshire and Gloucestershire. In 959 Saint Oswald was made bishop and he obtained a royal charter granting him and his successors jurisdiction over a large area of the surrounding country. Bishop Wulstan presided over the construction of a new cathedral, consecrated in 1084, which superseded the earlier timber building known to have been in existence in 680. Wulstan was the only Saxon bishop to retain his office after the Norman conquest. The present cathedral is largely later Norman work but Wulstan's crypt survives intact. Later alterations were made in 1225 and 1395.

King John was a frequent visitor to Worcester and directed that his body should be buried in the cathedral before the high altar. The beautiful medieval effigy carved in Purbeck marble, is the earliest likeness of a king in the country. It lies between the tombs of Saint Oswald and Saint Wulstan, whose prayers the king hoped might assist his progress through Purgatory. When the tomb was opened in 1797 the body was found to be wrapped in a monk's cowl.

The 14th century choir stalls contain a set of 37 misericords, a cartoon strip of daily medieval life. They are claimed by some to be the finest in England. An exquisitely carved Renaissance chantry tomb contains the body of Prince Arthur, eldest son of Henry VII, who died at Ludlow in 1502 at the age of 14, shortly after his marriage to Katherine of Aragon. Had he lived, there would have been no Henry VIII.

A town grew up around the cathedral which was walled from the 9th to 18th centuries. Only traces of the wall now remain. Franciscans arrived in Worcester in 1225 and in 1313 the old wooden bridge over the Severn was replaced by a stone one built by the monks. It must have been well-made - it lasted until the middle of the 18th century.

Friar Street has a number of timber-framed buildings and gives an impression of how medieval Worcester might have looked. Best of these is Greyfriars, a 15th century building which is an oasis of calm in the busy city and now belongs to the National Trust.

Worcester saw both the opening skirmish of the Civil War in 1642 at Powick Bridge and the final battle in 1651. The timber-framed Commandery which stands on the site of a hospital built by bishop Wulstan in 1085, served as Charles II's headquarters and is now a museum of the Civil War. In New Street (a continuation of Friar Street), King Charles' House was the scene of the king's escape through the back door as Parliamentary soldiers entered the front door.

Sunrise over Worcester Cathedral and the river Severn.

This photograph originally appeared in 'Worcestershire, A portrait of the county', published by Halfshire Books.

WORCESTERSHIRE

*The Cathedral from
Fort Royal Park.*

*Saint Wulstan's crypt,
the only surviving part
of the Cathedral he
consecrated in 1084.*

This photograph of the crypt
and of the quire screen originally appeared in
'Worcestershire, A portrait of
the county', published by
Halfshire Books.

The Queen Anne Guildhall of 1721, a very handsome building, makes clear its allegiance to the Royalist cause by displaying prominently above the entrance a carved stone effigy, said to be Cromwell's head, nailed by the ears.

Berrows Worcester Journal, first published in 1690, is the oldest newspaper in the country, and the Three Choirs Festival, held in rotation by the cathedral cities of Worcester, Hereford and Gloucester, has been a yearly event since 1720.

By the 18th century, Worcester had become a fashionable regional capital, full of elegant houses. Sadly, much was lost due to the combined effects of World War II and the subsequent activities of over-zealous town planners.

Entrance to the Cathedral quire, containing the tombs of King John, Prince Arthur, Saint Oswald and Saint Wulstan.

Friar Street. Greyfriars on the right of the picture above, left, was built in 1480 as a guest house for travellers. It belonged to the Fransiscan Friary next door, of which nothing now remains. Greyfriars is in the care of the National Trust.

King Charles House, from which the King fled on a borrowed horse, following his defeat by Cromwell's army.

The Duke of Hamilton, mortally wounded at the Battle of Worcester, was brought to the Commandery where he died.

Worcester to Bevere Lock

The footpath between Worcester and Bevere Lock has been colonised by Indian Balsam in a big way. It is everywhere, even spreading along one hedgerow inland away from the river, then making a right-angle turn, intent on enclosing the field with its outrageously camp shades of light and dark pink.

In a willow tree above the balsam I heard the unmistakable song of bullfinches. It is the only bird to my knowledge that sings a chord and is therefore easily identifiable, in spite of its secretive habit.

Bevere Island was used in the past as a refuge by the citizens of Worcester, first from the Danish raiders, then later the Civil War and the plague. Nearby is Camp House Inn which was licensed by Cromwell after the battle of Worcester.

This is perhaps a fitting point to say something about traffic on the river Severn. In the 17th century the river was navigable all the way from Welshpool to the sea. Fifty-foot long barges with a square sail could carry cargoes weighing up to fifty tons, while the larger trows were capable of carrying up to 90 tons. Trows were designed to overcome the problems posed by the river Severn's shifting sands and its variable depths of water. They were flat-bottomed with one, sometimes two, masts that could be lowered to pass under bridges. Where sails could not be used, they were pulled by gangs of men, between eight to twenty in number, called bow hauliers, wearing harnesses attached to a tow rope that was fastened to the top of the trow's mast. The banks of the river, unlike the canals, were not designed for this purpose and the men had to fight their way through bushes and scrub, wade through marshes and negotiate their passage round large trees. Harnessed like beasts and supporting themselves with one hand on the ground they slowly progressed up the river. Hard and occasionally dangerous men, they fiercely opposed the introduction of horses as replacements and in 1831 at Bewdley the riot act was read by a detachment of Scots Greys before order was regained.

Camp House Inn, about to be overwhelmed by Indian Balsam.

Old sand and gravel extraction quarry, left, reclaimed by nature, between Grimley and Holt.

Bevere Lock to Holt

Holt has a Norman church facing a castle with Norman origins, the oldest existing part being the 14th century tower. The church, dating from circa 1080, is one of the finest Norman churches in Worcestershire. Its exuberant decoration includes a beast biting its tail, a green man, a toothy monster, a fox and crane and a riot of zigzag arches.

It is a sobering thought that no construction or engineering project either before or since the Normans comes anywhere near to matching the breathtaking transformation of England that happened in the centuries immediately following the conquest. Formidable castles from one end of the kingdom to the other replaced the hastily-erected timber fortifications thrown up after 1066 and an amazingly ambitious programme of cathedral-building was begun. Great monasteries and abbeys appeared in remote and beautiful places. But most impressive of all, not content with all these major building projects, the Normans completely rebuilt almost every village church in the country. There are few old villages whose churches cannot trace their origins to the 12th century or even earlier. Many retain at least some Norman masonry if not a piece of sculpture.

Holt to Stourport-on-Severn

On a bitterly cold day but an extraordinarily good one for seeing wildlife, I walked from Holt to Stourport-on-Severn. Beginning with a kingfisher at Holt Lock, then two herons, I later saw five cormorants that had set up their winter quarters in the bare branches of riverside trees. Flapping away as I approached, they quickly settled in a tree a short way up river. No doubt the fishermen's keep nets remained empty until the birds moved on.

A big dog fox emerged from a thicket and loped off over a field. He knew I was there but whereas most foxes invariably make for cover as quickly as possible, this one, perhaps more confident than most owing to his size, kept pausing and staring at me. Eventually, having reached what he no doubt considered to be a safe distance, he sat down and watched me as I passed along the river bank. I saw two more foxes further on, the second with something white in its mouth. Returning a couple of hours later I noticed, from the shelter of a hedge, the same fox in the same place, again with something white in its mouth, moving purpose-fully across the field. This time, however, it stopped, placed the object on the grass and turned back. I walked over to look at it. It was a chicken. No doubt the fox was on its way back to steal another one.

A Spindle tree grows beside Holt Lock, covered in fiery red and yellow berries. Hedge-rows containing spindle trees are said to date at least from medieval times. The wood is particularly hard and was used for the weighted stick made for hand spinning raw wool before the invention of the spinning wheel. Skewers, pegs, knitting needles and toothpicks also are made from spindle tree wood. The fruits are a strong purgative.

On the western bank of the Severn, two miles or so upriver from Holt Lock, are Shrawley Woods, a hilly area of small-leaved lime trees, one of the few remaining refuges of the species in the country. In spring the woodland floor is carpeted with the delicate white flowers of wood anemones and followed soon after by great drifts of bluebells.

An ancient ford of the Severn was once in use nearby. It is difficult to visualise now, but before the river was deepened by the addition of locks to make it navigable, some stretches would have been much shallower.

Holt Castle has a 14th century tower and faces the church across a narrow unfenced road.

Exhuberant Norman carving at Holt Church.

Wood anemones in Shrawley woods are followed by bluebells making this one of the most delightful woods in the county.

The depth of the river Severn increased by five to six feet following the building of Lincomb lock and weir. When raised to half its height, the dam proved to be no match for the river's power, as five ton stones were rolled away. A solution to the problem was found by sinking canal boats loaded with stones. The lock was opened in 1844.

Hermits lived in rock caves in the woods and are credited with the rescue of unwanted babies set adrift in baskets up river at Bewdley. The hermits baptised and cared for the children until they were old enough to make their own way in the world. This might be rejected as an improbable folk tale were it not for the fact that the church registers of Shrawley and Abberley contain many people named Severne, one of whom was baptised Delarivere Severn (of the river Severn).

Further up river near Stourport-on-Severn, again on the western bank of the river, are the Redstone Caves. This also was once a much used ford and ferry crossing, originally the home of a single hermit, known to be there in 1160. He was later joined by monks on retreat from Worcester, who probably became keepers of the ferry. After the dissolution of the monasteries the caves went through a variety of uses, including that of ale house and only fell into disuse within living memory.

Stourport-on-Severn

Stourport-on-Severn owes its very existence to the genius of one man, James Brindley, the great 18th century canal engineer. Even the name of the place was different. Mytton was a sandy heath with a few farmhouses and one ale house at the confluence of the rivers Stour and Severn.

The barren heath became a flourishing town. Stourport-on-Severn was the great market place for the West Midlands. Coal, iron, grain, flour, hops, apples, salt, chinaware and other products arrived along the canal from Birmingham and the Black Country and were transferred to river-going vessels and sea-going ships while sugar, tea, spices and other foreign goods were transhipped by donkey or horse and cart inland. By 1796 the population of Mitton and Lickhill had grown to 1,300 inhabitants. The river was covered with trows and barges, the masts of the vessels looking like a forest of trees shorn of their leaves. Sometimes there were as many as sixty or seventy canal boats waiting their turn to pass into the canal for their journey up to the Black Country.

More basins were added until, by 1810, they were as large as they are today. In 1912, two more basins were added which have now been filled in, making seven basins in all.

Both the river Severn and the canal were very shallow and, at times, difficult to negotiate. Consequently, only three types of boat were seen at Stourport. The first was the magnificent trow, used only on the river, the second was the narrow boat, built for use on the canals, and the third was the barge, strictly speaking twice the width of a narrow boat and too large for most canals. The trows could be as long as 100 feet (approximately 30 metres) with a main mast and a top mast as high as 80 feet (24.38 metres). In 1797 28 trows were sailing weekly between Bristol and Stourport. The last trow was built in 1851 and named 'The Times'.

In the middle of the 1800s the Severn Steam Tug Company brought 'The Enterprise' from London. It could tow a line of ten or twelve barges from Stourport to Gloucester in 15 or 18 hours and was such a success that they ordered two more. The steam-driven tug began to replace the horses, despite their huge boilers and the large area needed to store

Barges in the Clock House basin.

a supply of coke. The first motor-driven tug arrived in 1930 with a little 14 hp engine.

From the 1830s onwards, as the prosperity of the canal waned, wages were lowered and the families of watermen began to make their homes aboard narrow boats as it became more and more difficult to pay the rent on the family house. People were born, lived and died on the boats. Because they were a mobile community, the Factory Acts and the Education Acts did not apply to them. The whole family, including the children often worked 18 hours a day for seven days a week as unpaid helpers.

Stourport-on-Severn, a history of the town and the area. Anne Bradford

A harmonious mixture of old and new buildings overlooking the Town Basin.

Evening beside the canal basins at Stourport-on-Severn.

Stourport-on-Severn to Bewdley

Only three miles or so apart, Bewdley is soon reached after leaving Stourport-on-Severn. On the way Blackstone Rock is passed, near to the modern bridge that carries the A456 Bewdley by-pass over the river. Blackstone Rock has many caves, homes for hermits in the distant past and, more recently, resting places for travellers on their way to Bewdley, waiting for an opportune moment to ford the river.

The legend of Blackstone Rock is repeated in various guises but while the personnel in each version may change the plot is very similar. A maiden elopes with, or is abducted by, a secret admirer. She is then killed by a henchman of her angry father, or by the man to whom she was formally betrothed. Her distraught lover retires to live the life of a hermit in the caves of Blackstone Rock where, many years later, he chances to hear the confession of her killer. The hermit then avenges the maiden's murder by throwing her killer from the crag to his violent death far below.

A rock-cut passage at Blackstone Rock.

Blackstone Rock, home of hermits and folklore beside the river Severn.

Bewdley

The first bridge over the Severn at Bewdley was constructed of stone in 1447, but was destroyed by Lancastrians during the Wars of the Roses. A timber bridge erected in 1461 lasted only a few years and was replaced in 1483 by a stone bridge with five arches, a toll house and a chapel. This lasted until 1795 when it was demolished by a great flood. The present bridge by Thomas Telford was erected in 1798 and is sited about thirty yards up-river from its predecessors.

A charter from the reign of Edward IV, dated 1447, gave Bewdley many privileges including that of sanctuary. Whispering Street (now Eastbourne Street) was where fugitives from justice waited under the bridge until darkness fell, when they would cross the river in a coracle or by the ford opposite Lax Lane. 'Lax' is derived from the Norse word for salmon, which was formerly so abundant in the river that articled apprenticeship documents included a clause saying that masters must not feed their apprentices salmon more than twice a week. Number 15 Lax Lane is the house where Stanley Baldwin, three times Prime Minister, was born.

The powerful Mortimers in the 15th century used the town as an administrative centre of the Council in the Marches of Wales before this was transferred to Ludlow. Just out of town is Tickenhill manor, once a great house often visited by royalty and the scene of the ill-fated Prince Arthur's marriage to Katherine of Aragon in 1499.

The town made a variety of goods but from the 15th century was best known for cap-making, an industry which, at its height, employed over 1,000 people. Merchandise coming up-river from Bristol was loaded on to pack-ponies and wagons to be distributed around the Midlands. It was not uncommon to see as many as 400 pack ponies tethered there. Many of the medieval houses were given a face-lift in the 19th century with brick facades, leaving the town with the Georgian appearance that we admire today.

During the Civil War Bewdley supported the king and the bridge became an important strategic defence. However, in 1644 Colonel Fox, leading a small detachment of Parliamentary soldiers, tricked his way into the town by shouting 'Make way for the Prince's regiment', adding that they needed quarter for the night. Five or six sentinels were killed and the town surrendered. He then led his troops to spring an even greater surprise on Tickenhill where there was a Royalist garrison under the command of Sit Thomas Lyttleton, a favourite of the King. The daring raid was a complete success and Lyttleton was carried off as a prisoner. Colonel Fox, however, did not profit from his military brilliance. Lyttleton was far too important to be ransomed by a mere colonel and was surrendered to Parliament, from where he soon found himself in the Tower of London.

In the great canal-building frenzy of the 18th century, Bewdley was one of seven towns that applied for a canal port, linking the canals to the river Severn. When their request was turned down in favour of Stourport-on-Severn, officials of the town declared that they hadn't wanted the 'stinking ditch' anyway.

19th century elections were lively affairs and none more so than at Bewdley where, in 1865, opponents of the Tory candidate had been offered £15 or as much rum and cider as they could drink if they changed their vote.

'At the rising of the sun frome the este the hole towne glittereth, being all of nuy buyldings, as it were of gold', reported Leyland of 16th century Bewdley. Merchants built their houses along Severnside, directly behind the quay which gave them easy access to river craft and the loading and unloading of a great variety of goods. Many of the houses were given a Georgian-makeover by later generations of occupants.

Load Street, Bewdley's short but busy main road.

Below, left:
The George Hotel in Load Street in its coaching days could stable over 40 horses. Engraved on one of the windows on the staircase is 'John Blome, 1777, March 4th, was hanged'.

The Old Butcher's Shambles, located underneath Bewdley's Town Hall, is now a museum dedicated to the town's history, which includes cap-making, tanning and rope-making.

The east bank of the Severn at Bewdley and the road to Kidderminster.

Severnside, up-river from the bridge has suffered in recent years from frequent flooding, causing much damage to furnishings in these small quayside houses. A system of removable barriers has now been installed which, it is hoped, will remedy the problem.

Bewdley to Upper Arley

The winter was mostly mild, but during the Christmas period, when I was walking between Upper Arley and Bewdley, a sudden dramatic change occurred with many days of freezing fog and severe ground frost, conditions which presented me with unusual photographic opportunities.

The whole landscape was locked in the iron grip of winter. Nature was silenced and nothing moved. Small groups of cattle huddled together for warmth, their steamy breath coiling slowly about their heads. From time to time the dense fog was penetrated by the distant swelling sound of steam engines puffing up the valley pulling carriages full of children and their parents on their way to meet Father Christmas at Upper Arley. The little country station was temporarily transformed into what surely must have been one of the busiest railway stations in England. There were crowds of people on the platforms, some wearing red woolly hats trimmed with white fur, while more disembarked from trains that seemed to be constantly arriving as others departed. Christmas music and electric lights pierced the fog, creating a noisy oasis of festive high spirits in the eerie winter white-out.

Upper Arley to Hampton Loade

Arley is perhaps the most charming of the stations on the Severn Valley Railway line and it was bliss to sit on a platform bench on a sunny day waiting for the steam engine and carriages to take me to Hampton, from where I would walk back along the bank of the river.

The line was built between 1858 and 1862 and linked Hartlebury with Shrewsbury. Although it provided an essential service to the area it was never financially successful and was closed during the 1960s. Happily a group of enthusiasts succeeded in saving the line which reopened in 1974. It is now the most popular line in England with regular train services operating between Kidderminster and Bridgnorth and possesses a large number of restored engines and carriages. Indeed, it is probably busier now than at any time in its history.

A big party of excitable young teenagers with a supervisor not much older, invaded the grassy bank behind the opposite platform. The station master's evident concern grew to anxiety as the time for the train's arrival approached. At last he called out saying that the opposite platform was closed and they should all come without delay over the road bridge to this side. A stampede followed.

Winter beside the river Severn at Upper Arley.

The Severn Valley Railway at Upper Arley station. This is the most popular preserved line in the country, with many restored locomotives and carriages. For much of its length between Kidderminster and Bridgnorth, the track follows the river valley.

The river Severn at Upper Arley. A ferry service, known to have been in use in 1323, was finally closed in 1971 when it was replaced by a rather undistinguished footbridge.

Upper Arley's 12th century church contains an effigy of a 14th century cross-legged armed knight, Walter de Balun, who had the misfortune to die from an accident in a tournament on his wedding day.

Right: A giant from the age of steam pulling carriages out of Stanley Station.

May blossom. Hawthorn is one of the commonest trees in the river's heartland,
due to its use as hedging at the time of the
Parliamentary Enclosures Acts.

An old trow, converted for use as a ferry at Coalport in the early nineteenth century.
It was replaced by a bridge in 1922. Ironbridge Gorge Museum Trust

THE RIVER **Severn**

SHROPSHIRE

Aimlessly, the river coils and uncoils its way from Wales

Hampton Loade to Bridgnorth

Again I chose to use the Severn Valley Railway to take me, this time, to Bridgnorth from Hampton Loade, from where I walked back along the river bank. Hampton Loade has the last working cable ferry on the river Severn, although I heard recently that it was no longer profitable and might be discontinued.

The village is mostly on the opposite side of the river, its most frequented building being the 14th century Lion Inn. An iron furnace and a brass foundry once flourished here and on hot summer days the workers were paid partly in beer.

Road access to Hampton Loade station is difficult, so for long periods the station appears to be deserted, but it comes alive when two trains arrive on opposite lines and railway staff busy themselves getting the trains on their way as passengers arrive and depart.

On the opposite platform, a family group, father, mother and two boys, were clearly, from their conversation, foreign visitors, probably Germans. The father had a camcorder and was video recording his wife and sons. A tall uniformed stationmaster complete with cap appeared, offered to take the camcorder and video the whole family. The father declined the offer. The stationmaster, however, was not to be denied and pursued the family across the tracks, all the time seeking to persuade the man of the benefits of a complete family group picture. (Whatever happened to English reserve?). Eventually the father gave in. The result, I suspect, was to be a scowl, a forced smile and two bored expressions.

There is a church above this cliff at Quatford that was built by Roger de Montgomery. It has a legendary foundation, described by Leyland, 'at the desyre of his wyfe that made a vow thereof in a tempest on the se'. Countess Adelisa, caught in storm at sea, vowed that if her life was spared, she would build a church on the spot where she had met her husband. Quatford was an important town at the time of Doomsday, it and Shrewsbury were the only Shropshire boroughs. However, Adelisa's son, Robert, abandoned the town and castle and moved to a better site at Bridgnorth in 1100. In earlier times the Danes had been troublesome raiders on and off for 100 years, but in 912 the Mercian queen, Ethelfleda, successfully fortified the area against attack.

Bridgnorth

The ruined keep of the castle built at Bridgnorth by Robert de Belleme, and behind it the church of Saint Mary Magdalene, designed by Thomas Telford and erected in 1792.

Although I have travelled through Bridgnorth and passed near to it on the by-pass hundreds of times, I must admit that before now I have never taken the trouble to stop and explore the town. By way of remedying the omission I decided to set aside a whole day for this purpose, and chose to travel there in style on the Severn Valley Railway from Kidderminster, rather than by car.

Mission accomplished and returning in the old-fashioned comfort of a carriage with a corridor and compartments, I reflected that for half a century and more I had missed out on one of England's best-kept secrets. Bridgnorth challenges Ludlow for the title of Shropshire's most attractive and unspoilt town.

Bridgnorth consists of a High Town built on top of a sandstone cliff and a Low Town at its foot, either side of the river Severn, the two sides being connected by a six-arched stone bridge built in 1823 that replaced an earlier eight-arched bridge and chapel.

The town was fortified in 912 by King Alfred's daughter, Ethelfleda, but its castle was built nearly two hundred years later in 1101-2 by Robert de Belleme, the son of Roger de Montgomery. It was destroyed by Cromwell's troops, who botched the job of blowing up the tower, leaving it at its present crazy and alarming angle.

The town has several narrow, picturesque streets, none more so than Cartway. This used to be the main road from High Town down to the bridge over the river and to the east. It is very steep and lined by many old and interesting houses, the best known of which is Bishop Percy's House near the bottom. This was built in 1580 and is timber-framed with three gables. For the pedestrian there is a choice of seven ancient steep stairways linking High to Low Towns.

Castle Street in High Town is an avenue of elegant Georgian houses ending with Telford's 1792 church as the focal point. High Street, the town's principle shopping street, was rebuilt after a fire and contains many attractive buildings housing shops, cafes and pubs, but the visitor's eye is likely to be caught first by the timber-framed town hall of 1650-52 standing in the centre of the road.

At one time Bridgnorth was second only in importance to Shrewsbury in the county, and had three dockyards, but that was in the days when the river was a main highway. The coming of the railways ended the town's prosperity.

Perhaps the town's best view (King Charles certainly thought so, declaring it be the finest in his kingdom) is from the Promenade along the High Town cliff edge, from where there is a bird's-eye view of the river and the bridge. This walk passes the station for the steepest funicular railway in the country, opened in 1892 and provides what is without doubt the easiest way to travel between High and Low Towns.

Castle Walk, High Town, follows the cliff edge, offering at one point a bird's eye view of the river Severn and the bridge.

The Swan, High Street. Most of medieval Bridgnorth was destroyed by fire in 1646 at the time of the Civil War. The fine half-timbered Town Hall in the centre of High Street was erected in 1652, but much of the town dates from the 18th century and is Georgian in style.

The bridge over the Severn at Bridgnorth. High and Low Towns are connected by a funicular railway, the steepest in England. A carriage can be seen in the photograph beginning its descent from High Town station.

Cartway, the very steep old main road from High Town to Low Town which leads to the bridge over the Severn.

Bridgnorth to Ironbridge

Apley Forge today is a sleepy backwater, giving little indication, apart from the name, that it was once a busy industrial site with two forges. A graceful white-painted suspension bridge erected in 1900 spans the river providing private access from Apley Hall to the former railway station, Linley, on the Severn Valley line. A Victorian Gothic mansion, Apley Hall, stands in the centre of parkland on the site of a former Georgian house which itself was erected on the site of a previous house built in 1308. The present house was built by a former Bridgnorth MP.

Only minor roads and lanes connect the Broseley to Bridgnorth road with the river bank, so this section of the route is particularly quiet. A group of donkeys gave me that characteristic melancholy look as I passed, made famous by AA Milne's 'Eyore'. Horses would have reacted with a sudden raising of the head and pricked ears. Cows would have stared intently and edged closer, full of curiosity. Sheep would scatter in panic, but donkeys look and look away, a take-it or leave-it expression and one can imagine them thinking, 'Just another human. He won't make our lives worse but then again, he won't make them better either!'

Some idea of the steepness of the hill on which Bridgnorth is built may be gained from the photograph above, left. A flight of steps beside these riverside houses begin their ascent to the distant church at the top of the hill.

This splendid merchant's house at the bottom of Cartway was built by Richard Forster in 1580. It is now known as Bishop Percy's House after a former occupant.

This majestic sandstone cliff called 'High Rock' is situated a short way up river from Bridgnorth

Rock-cut caves near Apley Forge. Caves like these, cut out of the red sandstone, are quite common in this area and were lived in as recently as the 1960's.

Ironbridge

At Ironbridge the Severn Way meets the Shropshire Way and briefly follows the same route. Soon, however, the latter heads north towards the Wrekin leaving the Severn Way to follow the river.

Until the 19th century, the river Severn was the main highway for all traffic through the West Midlands and the Welsh border. All manner of goods were carried on river craft between the sea and Welshpool, a distance of 160 miles.

The Ironbridge Gorge passes through an area rich in mineral deposits. Limestone, iron ore, coal, sand and clay are all to be found there. In the 16th century local landowners began to mine the coal for profit and tracks were laid to carry it to the banks of the river Severn.

By 1700 several furnaces, powered by water and fuelled by charcoal, were active and in 1709 a blast furnace in Coalbrookdale was leased by Abraham Darby in order to make iron, using coke as his fuel in place of the usual charcoal. His son Abraham Darby II constructed a blast furnace at Horsehay, and together with other ironmasters in the district, launched into a series of remarkable technological innovations that resulted in iron cylinders for steam engines, iron wheels for railway wagons, an iron barge for the river Severn - the first iron ship, pioneering the way for the ultimate iron ship, the SS Great Britain, whose wrought iron plates were made in Coalbrookdale.

The Iron Bridge, prototype for all subsequent steel-framed structures, was designed by Thomas Farnalls Pritchard, but the design was realised thanks to the technological inventiveness of Abraham Darby III. It took four years to build.

By the end of the 18th century about a quarter of all iron produced in the kingdom was coming from the Ironbridge gorge, but after 1810 its reputation declined and by 1870 the local trade collapsed.

The Ironbridge Gorge Museum is spread over six square miles and includes the following attractions: The iron bridge and toll house, the Darby furnace and Museum of Iron, the Bedlam furnaces, the Museum's Visitor Centre, a warehouse and wharf on the banks of the river Severn, Blists Hill Open Air Museum - a fifty-acre reconstruction of an industrial community in the late 19th century, the Coalport China Museum, the Jackfield Tile Museum, and the Hay Inclined Plane and Tar Tunnel.

The whole area, apart from the museums, is full of interest. Even some of the houses and garden walls are constructed with pieces of furnace slag and nodules of iron ore.

The walker, preparing to leave Ironbridge and studying a map of the area, may question whether the 'S' shaped ascent of Lincoln Hill is a worthwhile diversion from the Severn Way in order to reach Coalbrookdale, only five minutes walk down the road. Making his or her way through the hilltop woodland, past old limestone pits, these doubts, if still lingering, will be instantly dispelled, I'm sure, by the breathtaking view that is revealed on reaching a gap in the trees and the edge of a steep quarry. The leafy landscape of the Ironbridge Gorge and Benthall Edge is spread out below, with houses, half hidden by trees, clinging to the hillside, and tiny vehicles moving along the road beside the scene's dominant feature, the river Severn and its historic bridge.

The world's earliest surviving iron bridge, cast and constructed in 1779, a symbol of the pioneering technology of the 18th century in the Severn Gorge and Coalbrookdale. Today the whole area is a UNESCO designated World Heritage Site.

The Hay Inclined Plane. Barges were lifted between canals in wheeled cradles up this 1 in 3 gradient.

This level crossing, hidden among the trees, is a relic of the railway track that follows the south-west side of the Severn Gorge. The gate claims the distinction of being the widest in the country.

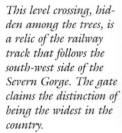

Coalport China Museum beside a short length of the Shropshire Canal that was built between 1788 and 1792.

Bedlam Furnaces, the subject of the famous painting 'Coalbrookdale by Night' by Philip James de Louthbourg, in which he captured the red sky, the flames and smoke, the noise and the intense activity around the furnace.

*Riverside shops and
houses near the iron
bridge at Ironbridge.*

Buildwas to Cressage

Summer happened in April in the year of this walk, and the ruins of Buildwas Abbey with its spacious mowed lawns was as good a place to be as anywhere in England. I stood at the back of the roofless nave looking towards the altar. The avenue of great Romanesque arches framed a cloudless blue sky and the sun cast black shadows on the lush green grass, where once there had been glazed patterned tiles. Founded in 1135 by the Cistercians, the surviving buildings date from c1200. It is a place of great serenity. But for me, it has also distant happy memories, for I passed it many times as a boy with my father as we walked from Buildwas Station on our way to the banks of the Severn for a day's fishing. Our journey from Birmingham by train always involved a lengthy wait for a connection at Wellington where we killed time by walking round the town, on one occasion finding a bakery from which we emerged with a bag of hot doughnuts. (My father lived on cakes when he was a boy and throughout his life never touched fruit or vegetables, apart from potatoes. Strangely, he filled his garden with all manner of fruits and vegetables, including apple, plum and pear trees. What happened to it all was a mystery).

The Chapter House, Buildwas Abbey.

The footpath in those days continued beyond the abbey ruins, beside the railway track, and past a farm underpass where once I saw a big grass snake slither away over the dusty ground and out of sight. Further on there were fields of ankle-length grass decorated with patches of Meadow Saffron or perhaps it was crocus depending on whether I saw the flowers in autumn or spring. That detail eludes me.

However, to return to the present. My tranquil hour or so at the abbey was interrupted by a little drama. A party of schoolchildren appeared, led by a young woman in a black sweater and followed by a young man. The woman was asking two of the girls their names. Suddenly a pupil shouted, 'Stop. Stand there!' A middle-aged man emerged from an archway and a heated exchange took place between the three adults ending with the older of the three saying 'You will be hearing more about this. It's disgraceful. You'd better get yourselves a good lawyer'. The young woman stormed off saying indeed she would be seeing a lawyer. It seemed as though I was witness to an audacious attempt at kidnapping. Next the rescuer of the children led them away to a bench and began to warn them about the dangers of trusting strangers. It was only when the young woman reappeared and joined the group that I realised it had all been a plot sprung on the children for educational purposes.

Incidentally, the April summer was followed by two months of Novemberish rain and wind.

The ascetic ideals of the early Cistercian Order are evident in the simplicity of the architecture of Buildwas Abbey. Unlike many other Cistercian abbeys that grew rich over the years on the produce of their vast estates, and spent lavishly on rebuilding in the latest architectural fashions, Buildwas Abbey was never altered. Much of the abbey's income came from the sale of wool that was shipped down the river Severn, but additional funds came from tolls levied on a nearby bridge. Little seems to have disturbed the well-ordered lives of the brothers throughout the abbey's existence, apart from the murder of an abbot in 1342 by one of the monks.

Nature's fan vaulting in Piners Coppice. The footpath climbs out of the valley through these attractive woods and emerges on to a road leading to Cressage.

A loop of the river Severn seen from Leighton Park.

Cressage to Atcham

Cressage derives its name from Cressage Oak or Christ's Oak, so it seems not unreasonable to accept as fact that the great oak tree that once stood at the centre of the crossroads, on the spot now occupied by the war memorial, was indeed the tree under which Saint Augustine preached to the Welsh Bishops in AD 584.

There is a link between Cressage and Holt in Worcestershire, which I passed on this walk many miles back. An oak tree in Holt's churchyard is grown from an acorn taken from the Cressage Oak.

Viroconium was the fourth largest Roman town in Britain. Only a relatively small area of the site has been excavated and the rest lies awaiting rediscovery under the green fields of modern Wroxeter.

Two Roman pillars now act as gateposts to the churchyard and the upturned base of a massive Roman column inside the Saxon church serves as its font. Part of the nave is constructed using Roman masonry, whilst high above the entrance can be seen the remains of Saxon carving in the form of part of a fine cross shaft and two animal fragments. European history and the early history of England are fused in this unlikely setting, a parish church in a sleepy Shropshire village.

Other bits of Roman masonry put to modern use can be found if one peers over hedges into private gardens. Even a humble half-timbered cottage displays a section of Roman pillar, now in use as a gatepost, beside its narrow roadside garden.

Viroconium had defences enclosing an area of 200 acres. Much remains to be investigated, but the basilica, the bath, market hall and forum may be viewed as well as finds displayed in a small on-site museum. Roman Watling Street crossed the Severn here, and fragments of a timber bridge have been found on an island in the river. Today, vineyards flourish within the boundary of the Roman defences, producing one of the world's most northerly red wines, as well as white.

d Work' is the name
uired by the tallest
ion of wall still
nding, seen here
inst the setting sun.

teen bases of columns
a trench, far right,
the remains of a
nnade that formed
t of the city forum.

Re-used Roman columns beside the entrance gates at Wroxeter's Saint Andrew's church.

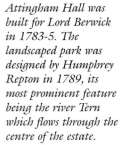

Attingham Hall was built for Lord Berwick in 1783-5. The landscaped park was designed by Humphrey Repton in 1789, its most prominent feature being the river Tern which flows through the centre of the estate.

Part of a Saxon cross shaft with an indeterminate beast and vine scroll, and a separate carving of an animal, now incorporated into the south wall of Wroxeter's church.

Atcham, where they catchem' my fisherman father used to say. The river is exceptionally wide at Atcham, making one wonder why this was the spot chosen to build not one, but three successive bridges. The first was erected by the Abbot of Lilleshall in 1222 and has long been gone. The bridge built in the 1770s, made redundant by the one in use now from the 1920s, has happily been preserved and the two can be seen side by side. Of the two, the one in use today lacks the confident flair of its redundant neighbour, failing to match the older bridges' assured elegance.

Perhaps the great width of the river at Atcham is a clue to this choice of crossing. Wide rivers are often shallow rivers, so before anyone thought of constructing a bridge it may have been used for centuries as a safe ford over what elsewhere is a deep and dangerous river.

Much older than either bridge is the church, dedicated to Saint Eata, the only one in Britain with this dedication. Saint Eata, a Celt, was consecrated Bishop of Lindisfarne in AD 678 and the church at Atcham was built in the 11th century. Its Saxon north wall contains re-used masonry from nearby Roman Viroconium. Some blocks have dovetail holes to take a Roman lifting machine.

John Gwynn's elegant 1770s bridge at Atcham and behind it, its replacement, the concrete bridge erected by Salop County Council in the late 1920s.

Saint Eata's church, Atcham, one of Shropshire's earliest surviving buildings. Ordericus Vitalis, a monk who wrote a history of the Normans in 1075, was baptised in this Anglo-Saxon church.

Preston Boats. A rope ferry used to operate here, but it and the old fish weir belonging to nearby Haughmond Abbey have both gone. A short stroll up river from Preston Boats brings the walker to the site of another vanished ferry at Uffington. The First World War poet, Wilfrid Owen, lived at Monkmoor on the edge of Shrewsbury and he and his family would often cross on the ferry to worship in Uffington village church.

Atcham to Shrewsbury

My father was an enthusiastic, though not particularly successful, fisherman. Preston Boats and Buildwas were his favourite stretches of water. Getting to either, however, from Birmingham where we lived, involved a bus journey from the suburbs to Snow Hill Station, followed by a train ride (two trains for Buildwas) and ending with a lengthy walk to the river bank. The trips were enlivened by a long-running feud between the railway company's staff on the one hand and the fishermen on the other. The latter had discovered that if they bought a workman's return ticket from Birmingham to Wolverhampton and a further workman's return ticket from Wolverhampton to Shrewsbury, the overall cost of the fare could be greatly reduced. The railway staff, aware that this abuse of the system was regularly happening, declared war on the fishermen and chose Wolverhampton as the battlefield. As the train pulled into Wolverhampton station, carriage doors would open and the fishermen would jump out, the train still being in motion, and race to the ticket kiosk to get their workman's return ticket to Shrewsbury. Whereupon the man behind the desk would be struck by an inexplicable attack of lethargy. Meanwhile, out on the platform, a red-faced guard was racing up and down the platform, slamming doors and harrying passengers into the carriages, his single-minded ambition being to get the train away leaving as many fishermen behind as possible.

I remember clearly as a young boy, nervously holding open the carriage door while my father took part in this pantomime, and wondering what would become of me and the compartment full of fishing tackle if the train went without him.

A bridge at Preston Boats carries the railway track over the river Severn and here sometimes the train would be held up by signals. When this happened, carriage doors flew open to reveal the parachute regiment of the Birmingham Anglers Association, leaping out and scrambling down the embankment, happy to be so quickly beside the river and saved from the tedious long walk from the centre of Shrewsbury.

A rope stretching across the river at Preston Boats was the means by which a flat-bottomed ferry boat, like a punt, passed from bank to bank. On the far side there is a farm house. Fishermen would hail the ferrywoman and order a hot dinner, and a little later this would duly arrive by boat and be paid for.

Winters in the days of my childhood seemed to be a lot colder than now. I recall sitting on the banks at Preston Boats one bitterly cold day, watching great chunks of ice floating past. It may have been the same winter that my father returned home one evening with a bag full of roach and chubb, wrapped in damp rags. Amazingly, they were all still alive. A galvanised bath was quickly filled with water and the fish soon recovered.

I count myself lucky to have survived those fishing trips. The banks of the river Severn are high and steep. Rough steps, hacked out by fishermen, descend to river level where my father would settle me down on my creel before moving off to his own chosen spot. The tiny ledge on which I was perched was often very muddy and it would have been easy to slip and fall into the river. Deep along much of its length the river Severn is notoriously dangerous with powerful currents. Neither my father nor I could swim. It is more than fifty years since I was last at Preston Boats, and being there again brought back many memories.

Shrewsbury

The first written evidence for the existence of Shrewsbury is in a charter of 901 referring to 'Scrobbesbyrig', a scrub-covered fortified hill. By Anglo-Saxon times the town had grown large enough to include five churches, and during the reign of Athelstan a mint was established which continued to strike coins for the next 300 years.

Most of Shropshire, including Shrewsbury, was granted by William the Conqueror to Roger de Montgomery, and was held by successive Norman earls until 1125 when the town was presented by Henry I to his second wife who appointed William Fitz Alan as her deputy. In 1189, Richard I granted the oldest surviving charter giving the burgesses the town in return for payment to the king of forty marks of silver each year.

A succession of English kings used Shrewsbury throughout the 13th century as an important base from which to launch attacks against the Welsh. The town was also involved in the civil war between Henry III and the barons led by Simon de Montfort who stayed there with his army in 1264. One year later the town was host to the king's army.

In 1277 and 1282 Edward I passed through Shrewsbury with his forces on his way to fight Llewelyn, Prince of Wales, who had refused to do homage to him and was destined to die on the field of battle. Llewelyn's successor, David, was captured the following year and subsequently tried and executed in Shrewsbury.

By the 14th century Shrewsbury was one of the dozen richest towns in England and the population is believed to have grown to about 3,000. The town's guildsmen included shoemakers, metalworkers, tanners, glovers, skinners, workers in horn and stone, drapers, shearmen, mercers, tailors, archers, armourers, a bowyer, a fletcher and a dealer in parchment.

Shrewsbury continued to play a prominent part in the interminable feuds between rival claimants for the throne of England, and between the Welsh and the English. In 1485 Richard III lost his life and his crown on Bosworth Field and so began 150 years of Tudor peace and prosperity, which was to benefit this town as it did many others in the kingdom. New crafts flourished, feltmakers, coopers, brickmakers and pewterers practised their skills, as did upholsterers and weavers, chandlers and vintners. The river Severn became an important waterway for cloth and other goods from Wales passing though the town on their way down river to Bristol or by packhorse to London.

In 1552 the grammar school was founded, an early scholar being Sir Philip Sydney. By 1832 when it was visited by the future Queen Victoria, then aged 13, it had become a major public school, Charles Darwin being perhaps its most famous pupil. In the late 17th century the population had increased to nearly 7,500 and included fifty tailors, twelve barbers, nine tobacconists, six watchmakers, dancing masters, milliners, booksellers, a bookbinder, a furrier and a perfumer to serve the needs of increasingly fashionable visitors and residents.

By the end of the 18th century Shrewsbury had become what it remains today, probably the best medieval town in the country. Apart from the loss of its finest church, St Chads, which collapsed in 1788, it has happily, unlike many other towns, preserved its best and most attractive buildings. Throughout the 18th and 19th centuries further buildings were erected which, though in completely different styles of architecture, managed nevertheless to harmonise effortlessly with their earlier neighbours.

Fish Street is as narrow as it looks in this photograph. The cobbled lane passes many half-timbered houses on its way to Saint Julian's church, seen in the distance. Bear Steps, a gateway through a modern restoration of a 14th century hall house, leads to Saint Alkmund's churchyard. The church spire is just visible above the house roofs.

Jettys, almost meeting like an avenue of trees, above Fish Street near its junction with Butcher Row.

Five Anglo-Saxon churches were founded in Shrewsbury before the Norman conquest, among them Saint Mary's in circa 960. It was rebuilt in the late 12th century. The 14th century Jesse window is much travelled., having previously been in Saint Chad's Church and before that, probably in Greyfriars. A notice beside a church door informs the reader that the church is open on weekdays but closed on Sundays! Truly a sign of the times.

This carved figure is of Richard, Duke of York, father of Edward IV. It was moved to its present position commanding a view of the market place from the tower of the old Welsh bridge in 1791.

The Square, right. The site of Shrewsbury's market since 1269, this area has remained the traditional focal point of the town. Surrounded by fine houses, the Old Market Hall was where the Drapers conducted their business in the upper room. Folklore says that the wool market collapsed when Welsh merchants, bringing their cloth to Shrewsbury, eventually realised they were being cheated.

Below: one of many handsome buildings in Mardol.

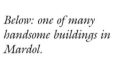

The King's Head Inn, Mardol, below right, was a 14th century merchant's house.

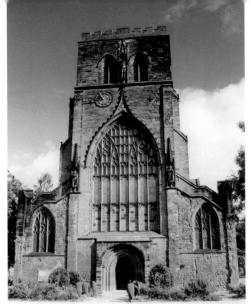

Founded in 1083 by Roger de Montgomery, The Abbey, a Benedictine monastery, was completed early in the 12th century.

Houses at the bottom of Wyle Cop.

The English Bridge of 1769. In Leyland's time a bridge was here with four great arches and a drawbridge.

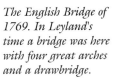

Wyle Cop, the oldest street in Shrewsbury and still one of the busiest. The house on the right of the picture, Henry Tudor House, is where Henry VII stayed before the battle of Bosworth in 1485.

Shrewsbury to Montford Bridge

The Severn Way leaves Shrewsbury along a very narrow footpath that cuts through steep terraced gardens backing on to the river. The walk would be pleasant and interesting (prying into other peoples' back gardens is a rare treat) were it not for the fact that the path was fouled with dog turds every few paces. My eyes were therefore fixed on my feet rather than the gardens.

This narrow footpath gives way to the deepest holloway I have ever seen, with enormous old trees growing on either bank, their crowns mingling to make a tunnel full of dappled light and shade. My guess is that it was once long ago the main route for traffic out of Shrewsbury before it was made redundant by the construction of modern roads.

Montford Bridge to Wilcott Marsh

There has been a bridge spanning the Severn at Montford since the early Middle Ages. The present one is by Thomas Telford and was erected in 1792. An ancient river crossing and meeting place for negotiations between English and Welsh leaders in warlike times, this was the site of a notorious act of treachery when, in 1283, Dafydd ap Gruffudd, the last prince of Wales, was handed over to the English in chains by his own countrymen. The usual formality of a trial resulted in the usual barbaric execution.

There is much road-walking along little-used lanes in this part of the route, but it is compensated for by fine views of the distant Shropshire hills and the Brieddens and a variety of wild flowers either side of the tarmac. Birdsfoot Trefoil, Evergreen Alkanet and Fumitory, a plant unfamiliar to me, caught my attention, as did Mountain Cranesbill which was everywhere. Indeed it confirmed my growing suspicion that the self-seeded plant I had lovingly cared for all last summer in a clay pot was in fact this weed. No matter, it is a pretty flower.

The churches at both Montfort and Shrawardine are built with red sandstone which has eroded so badly that it makes one wonder if sandstone is a suitable choice of material for permanent buildings - Montford church was erected in 1737-8 and is therefore less than three-hundred years old. Buried near the tower are the remains of Robert Darwin and his wife Susannah Wedgwood, daughter of Josiah Wedgwood, the potter. They were the parents of the famous Charles Darwin.

Shrawardine castle was built soon after the conquest but was destroyed by the Welsh in 1215. Rebuilt after 1220, it was dismantled by Cromwell's army in 1645 after a five-day siege. The little that remains today is being carefully preserved and is a ruin typical of the Welsh Marches.

Wilcott Marsh to Melverley

The road-walking continues, apart from a mile or so near Pentre where the route takes to the fields. I should have learned by now that grass in summer is very different to grass in winter. Winter grass is springy turf. Easy on the feet, it speeds you on your way, but by summer it has grown knee high and is like wading through treacle.

Valerian grows in ditches beside the road and in the distance I heard the haunting cry of a curlew.

Saint Chad's church, Montford. An island in a bend of the river Severn at Montford is the site of a fish weir which is known to have been in use as early as the late 11th century. The weir stretched from side to side of the river, causing an obstruction to river traffic, so a bypass was dug, creating an island. Forty such weirs were recorded in Shropshire in the 16th century but most had fallen into disuse by the end of the 1600s. Montford's weir was one of the last at the time of its demise in the late 1800s.

A toll house near to Thomas Telford's bridge over the river Severn at Montford Bridge.

he river Severn at
rawardine,
nsiderably shrunk in
dth compared to
rewsbury a few miles
wn stream.

One of only two timber-
framed churches in
Shropshire. Saint Peter's
at Melverley stands
right on the border of
England and Wales.
The parish was part of
the Welsh diocese of
Saint Asaph until the
1920s when it was
transferred to Lichfield.

Buttercups, possibly the most familiar and abundant flower of riverside meadows.

An illustration of Pool Quay made sometime before the middle
of the nineteenth century. This was the highest navigable point on the river.
Powysland Museum and Montgomery Canal Centre

THE RIVER Severn
POWYS·WALES
Mountain stream and infant river

Melverley to Offas Dyke Path

Melverley has a rare example of a timber-framed wattle and daub church, its interior more like a barn than a church. All the original oak beams are fixed together with wooden pegs. There was a chapel at Melverley before the Norman Conquest, but it was destroyed in 1401 by Owain Glyndwr. By 1406 the present church, containing the original Saxon font, was in use. It is in a charming, if perilous, situation, perched on the very edge of the afon Efyrnwy and consequently is often cut off by flood water.

A short walk from the church, the Seven Way passes the confluence of the afon Efyrnwy and the river Severn, or, to give it its Welsh name as the route has here crossed the border, the afon Hafren. The Breidden Hills, a distant feature on the horizon from Montford Bridge, increasingly dominate the scenery as the walk gets progressively closer. They are now a dark and brooding presence, shutting off the view to the south and east. All three summits have iron-age fortifications.

I rubbed my eyes in disbelief near Lower House Farm. The fields were full of water buffalo, some of them wallowing in rather inadequate muddy depressions, presumable excavated by the farmer for their benefit. All of the beasts were plastered up to their bellies with grey mud.

The Severn Way guide book describes as 'easy walking' the route along the top of the flood bank up-river from Llandrinio. No doubt it is from winter to spring, but in June, once again I found myself floundering along in an endless sea of knee-high grasses. I was feeling tired, and had another two-and-a-half hours walking ahead of me to reach my car, followed by up to two hours of driving home. Nevertheless, on the strength of the guide book's mention of part of a carved cross shaft in the porch of Llandrinio church, I made a short detour. The outer porch door, one of the heaviest solid oak doors I have ever seen, was firmly shut and locked.

119

Cows cooling off on a warm afternoon in the river Severn, now the Welsh Hafren near Crew Green.

The Breidden Hills and the afon Hafren.

New Cut, left, and sluice gates, right, both help to control floodwater in the broad flatlands down river from Welshpool.

Moel-y-Golfa, the most southerly of the Breidden Hills.

Offa's Dyke Path to Welshpool

The Severn Way joins the Offa's Dyke path near Llandrinio and leaves it about three miles up-river, where, at Pool Quay, it follows the canal towpath.

This part of the Offa's Dyke path was dismissed in the published guide book as being flat and without interest. It even suggested the walker might like to bypass it and resume the walk further north. I ignored this advice and was glad that I had, for the countryside, although flat, was made interesting by the long, raised flood barriers, water-filled dykes and great gates for controlling the river when in flood. Confidence in my decision to ignore the guide's advice was confirmed when I regained the historic Offa's Dyke and found it covered in primroses.

The Mercian King Offa reigned from 757 to 796. He was the first ruler to be styled king of the English, having achieved unprecedented power by murdering in 793 Aethelbert, King of East Anglia, who was his guest. After years of strife on his Welsh border Offa gained temporarily the upper hand and in approximately 784 the Dyke, which in Bishop Asser's phrase, ran 'from the sea right to the sea' was constructed.

Its purpose was as a frontier from where trade could be controlled. Generally the Dyke consists of a bank to the east with a ditch to the west and the maximum height in the best-preserved sections can be as much as thirty feet. Its effectiveness was limited however, as the mixture of English and Welsh place names either side of the earthwork suggest. Even recently someone could be referred to as having been born 'the wrong side of the Dyke', casting doubt on their allegiance.

Built in the early years of the 19th century, the Montgomery Canal, also known as the Shropshire Union Canal, was used for the transportation of limestone from quarries at Llanymynech, and timber, grain and dairy products. Its working life effectively ended in 1935, since when it has progressively become a haven for wild life.

The afon Hafren flows under Buttington bridge near to Welshpool. Here, in ancient times, there was a ford, the Rhyd-y-groes, where, according to the Welsh *Mabinogion* 'a great host of king Arthur gathered on a flat island below the ford'. The Anglo-Saxon Chronicles record a battle fought in 894 between the Saxons and the Danes. The Saxons won, but a hundred years later, they were themselves beaten here by the Welsh. In the 19th century, workmen digging foundations for the new school uncovered three pits containing bones and a display of 350 skulls was arranged in the nearby church.

Rhyd-y-groes was also forded by Henry Tudor and his army in 1485 when he was on his way to Shrewsbury and his destiny at the Battle of Bosworth.

he Montgomery canal Pool Quay. Pool Quay as the highest avigable point on the on Hafren although ly in winter was this ssible due to the extra pth of the water. With flannel mill, lead works nd warehouses it was a ace of some importance. he building of the nal provided a more liable means of ansport and by the iddle of the 19th ntury the use of the

river for commerce had ended. The site of Strata Marcella, a Cistercian abbey founded in 1170, is nearby. It was in its day a flourishing abbey with far-flung possessions, but all trace of it disappeared long ago.

The Montgomery canal near Welshpool.

Welshpool

Halfway between Pool Quay and Welshpool, a field lying between the canal and the Afon Hafren is the site of Strata Marcella, a Cistercian Abbey founded by Owain Cyfeiliog in 1170. In its day the monks enjoyed grazing rights as far away as Plynlimon, unlimited supplies of charcoal from the forests, lead workings in the hills, a windmill, and water power from the abbey's weir on the river. The first abbot, Enoch, intended to found a house for Cistercian nuns at Llansantffraid, but he fell in love with one of the women and together they eloped. It was a great scandal and the nunnery was never realised.

The original Welsh name for Welshpool was Y Trallwng after the pool near the castle. The English 'Pool' tended to be confused with Poole in Dorset so in 1835 it became Welshpool. The town was granted its market charter in 1263, 60 years after the building of nearby Powis Castle.

Powis Castle belonged to the princes of Powis until the 13th century when the last prince, Gwenwynwyn, also known as Lord de la Pole, was summoned to Shrewsbury to surrender his name and crown to the English king. From that day he and his heirs' status was reduced to that of a feudal baron of England. He died in 1293 when the castle was valued at £2 4s 4d.

A descendent, Sir Edward Herbert, spent a huge sum, refurbishing the castle in 1587. The Long Gallery and state bedrooms were added after the Civil War, and the grounds were landscaped in the early 19th century by Capability Brown. The castle today is owned by the National Trust and is renowned for its 300 metre long terraced gardens, laid out originally in the 18th century.

Welshpool's Old Railway Station, surplus to requirements, has been converted for use as a shopping centre, its preserved platform alarmingly separated from the rail track which has been moved to the far side of the busy A483.

Three long-distance footpaths meet at or very near to Welshpool, Offa's Dyke Path, Glyndwr's Way and the Severn Way.

Left: two customers enjoy a pint as they watch the world go by outside The Mermaid in the High Street, Welshpool.

High Street, Welshpool.

'Hopkins Passage leading to Puzzle Square', announces an antique sign above the narrow entrance to this twisting alley.

Nineteenth-century civic pride expressing itself in imposing public buildings is found in the centre of Welshpool as in many other Welsh towns.

'Grace Evans Cottage', right. Her claim to fame is due to the help she gave the earl of Nithsdale in 1716 when he was a prisoner in the Tower of London. She exchanged clothes with him and assisted him and the countess to escape to the Continent. Grace Evans returned to Wales in 1735.

Named after the famous Montgomery Oak that once grew at the cross roads, the Royal Oak may stand on the site of the Earl of Powis's manor house. This building dates from the early 1700s.

A listed building, The Old Station, right, houses shops selling ladies' wear, men's wear, gifts, souvenirs, a golfers' shop and a restaurant.

The Tower of Saint Mary's Church. Founded by Saint Gynfelyn in 542, the church was rebuilt in 1275 and again in 1866. Its panelled roof is thought to have come from Strata Marcella, as does the stone called Maen Llog opposite the church door. This stone had been used as a throne by the abbey's abbot, but it was thrown out of the church by Parliamentarian soldiers during the Civil War.

Opened in 1990, the Powysland Museum and Montgomery Canal Centre occupies a former warehouse beside the canal. Its collection includes artefacts gathered by a group of local enthusiasts who in 1867 formed a club for those who were interested in the history of mid-Wales.

Welshpool to Fron

The canal Z-bends under the A490 south of Welshpool and, on emerging from the low cement-ceilinged tunnel, I found that my progress along the narrow towpath was barred by two swans and their cygnets. No amount of encouragement or flapping of arms would persuade them to give way and enter the water. And who could blame them? It was a sunny day, they were resting and this was their territory, not mine. I backed off and was lucky to find an alternative path that returned me to the canal about 50 yards past the swans.

The commonest bird apart from ducks on this stretch of the canal seems to be herons. I have never seen so many in one place before. But although the water in the canal is clear and not very deep I saw no fish.

A car passed me with a bunch of heather fastened to the front of its bonnet, a sight I have not seen for many years, although it used to be very common. At one time some cars had so much of the stuff that they looked as though they had been involved in an accident and careered off the road into the purple wilderness, emerging heavily-disguised and ready for jungle warfare. The custom was a cheap and easy way to announce to the world that the occupants had recently returned from a holiday in Scotland. These days everyone goes to the Algarve or Cyprus or Barbados, so the custom has died out.

Were it not for the busy A483 which never strays far from the canal, this would be a very tranquil and charming part of the Severn Way. The canal is well-maintained, although no longer in use for the purpose for which it was built. The towpath weeds and brambles appear to be controlled and sections of the bank have been repaired using modern technology. Even the locks are in good condition, although apparently never used. This is due to the fact that in several places roads now cut through the canal, forming barriers only a few yards wide and so preventing boats from travelling along what would otherwise be largely a navigable water-way apart from short stretches below Welshpool.

I saw no sign of the basking grass snakes or kingfishers that the guide book promises but I did see an abundance of dragonflies, mostly Common Blue Damselflies, more often than not riding tandem. I also saw a spectacular example of a Brown Hawker dragonfly with a pale, bronze-coloured body and bronze, translucent wings. Amazing metallic stardust markings flashed in the sunlight as it patrolled the towpath ahead of me.

A spectacular hedge of everlasting sweet pea separates a garden and house from the canal towpath between Berriew and Garthmyl. The riot of fuchsia and pink blooms made me envious. I have tried unsuccessfully to grow this plant at my home for the last three years and every time it succumbs to a virus.

Boot problems. I decided to reduce the overall load by wearing some old cheap light-weight canvas boots with moulded soles and heels. Last year I discovered the folly of buying this footwear when a sharp stone punctured one of the hollow heels, letting in water. As there had been no rain for a week I reckoned that my foot would remain dry. However, by the time I was halfway back to my car, and in spite of a day of easy towpath-walking, the paper thin soles of the boots had provided virtually no support to my feet and my bones felt as though they had suffered some sort of unwelcome rearrangement. Sturdy leather boots were my choice of footwear for the remainder of the journey.

cottage garden hedge
sweet peas beside the
nal.

Cows slake their thirst
with water from the
canal on a hot
afternoon near Belan.

Fron to Llanllwchaiarn

A lone fisherman greeted me as I approached along the canal towpath. Behind him the rushing water of the afon Hafren tumbling over little waterfalls and across shallow beds of stones, contrasted markedly with the nearly motionless water of the narrow canal. Only a few yards separated the two. Why, I wondered, did he choose to fish in the canal rather than the river? 'Is it good fishing in the canal?' I asked. 'It is if you want to catch pike' he replied. 'There are lots of pike in here. They feed on the small stuff, mostly roach. There's not much else though!'.

When I last was beside the Hafren, near Llandrinio, in the shadow of the Breidden hills, it was a typical lowland river. Slow moving, deep, and with high vertical banks. At Newtown it is wide and changeable, sometimes shallow, with rapids, sometimes deep and moving more slowly but unmistakably an upland river.

At Abermule a swan once again was blocking my progress along the towpath. It was alone, and did not appear to be concerned by my approach. However, as I edged past, it turned on me, pursuing me along the path with wings outstretched and hissing from a beak that lunged on the end of an s-shaped neck. Passing through a little gate I was glad to be rid of it. Moments later though, a thunderous beating of wings made me spin round to confront a white missile with a five foot wingspan. It crashed, noisily, into the canal a few feet away and swam beside me as I walked, fixing me with its hostile, beady little black eye. Further on, two swans with cygnets, fortunately in the water, told me to clear off, also with much hissing.

Later on the towpath I nearly fell over a pale brown hen pheasant with her brood of pretty little chicks. She was startled by my sudden appearance and after scolding me (it was a great day for hostile birds) flew to the other side of the canal, abandoning her chicks to their fate. They, meanwhile, were quickly disappearing into the long grass. I hastened on, knowing that the pheasant would soon return to her brood when she was sure I was gone.

Dolforwyn Castle, according to the OS Landranger map, is close to the canal, in the hills facing Abermule. A CADW publication called 'Great Castles' allows it a brief mention and its existence was confirmed by a young woman in 'Tourist Information' at Llanidloes. So it was quite frustrating when I failed utterly in my search for the place. At one point, coming across a very small official-looking car park at the top of a pass, I thought I had cracked it, but apart from a very steep rough track leading to a house high on the hill, there was no sign of an entrance or visible remains of a castle. The car park seemed to serve no purpose and only deepened the mystery.

Determined not to be beaten, when I returned home I made telephone enquiries and, as a result, received in the post from the Countryside Commission a photocopied leaflet showing a guided walk. Unfortunately it was so badly printed that half the information was illegible.

However, a week later I was again on my way in search of Dolforwyn Castle. Motoring along the A483 and nearing the junction of the lane leading into the hills I was surprised to see conspicuous yellow signs, marked 'Dolforwyn Castle' with an arrow. These were repeated at every junction, and led me to the little four-bay car park that I had observed the previous week. This time, however, the road was blocked by two minibuses, a car and a

Dolforwyn Castle, buil *by the Welsh in 1273,* *was captured by the* *English a mere five* *years later.*

The English captors of Dolforwyn hacked through 21 feet of solid rock to reach the water supply for this well.

Brynderwen locks and cottage. This was formerly a canal wharf with a 19th century warehouse which can still be seen.

crowd of about twenty people. Squeezing past, I parked my car and noted that a smart new permanent sign had appeared offering a brief history of the castle.

More directional signs, pointing up the steep track that I had noticed before, led past the house to the castle ruins. Puffing up the hill, I was passed by two 4x4s on their way down, but on reaching the site I was pleased to see that I had it all to myself.

The castle's appeal for the modern visitor must be its airy position on the rocky summit of a wooded hill that falls away steeply on all sides. It was built in 1273 by Llewelyn ap Gruffud and was the last castle to be built by a prince of Wales. In 1277 or 1279 it was besieged by a small English army led by Roger Mortimer and Henry de Lacy and surrendered after eight days of battering with siege engines.

The Welsh had relied on rainwater for their needs but the new owners cut through 21 feet of solid rock to reach water. The rectangular well, full to the brim with greenish water, and sheltered by an arch, is one of the site's most interesting features.

Although most of the walls are only a few feet high, the castle is well worth the climb. Much work has gone into its preservation and it is sensitively furnished with olive green metal stairs, rails and barriers.

A young man engaged me in conversation beside the well. It transpired that he had been a member of the company responsible for the manufacture and installation of the metal walkways. It was impossible, he said, to get either a crane or truck up to the top of the hill, and all the metalwork had to be manhandled by eight men using brute strength. The crowd of people at the car park, he confirmed, had been to the castle's official opening day.

The constant roar of traffic on the Welshpool to Newtown road, between Fron and Abermule, where the canal and road are separated only be a fence or hedge, is very disagreeable. I was growing tired of canal walking after three days, and looked forward to fresh scenery as the Severn Way takes to the hills above Newtown.

The Montgomery canal's ignominious end near Newtown.

Newtown, from a spectacular vantage point on the Kerry Hills.

Newtown

The best view of Newtown is gained from a narrow road that hugs the edge of the top of hills between the town and Kerry. From this vantage point the full extent of the sprawling, mainly modern town of housing estates and light industry, is very evident. This is the largest town in mid-Wales.

Newtown was 'new' in 1279, when Roger Mortimer was granted a market charter for the formerly-named Llanfair Cedewain. It was laid out in the usual grid pattern and Glyndwr's court poet described it as 'a municipality regulated like Paradise'.

As elsewhere in the region, the basis of its prosperity was sheep. Newtown is overlooked by the Kerry Hills, grazing grounds for the Kerry sheep, a breed with a white face, black nose and black knees, renowned for their soft white wool. The sound of spinning wheels could be heard at nearly every cottage door in times past. The building of the Montgomeryshire canal stimulated trade and the town grew ever more prosperous as wool production was taken over by factories.

Dominating the town, the 19th century Royal Welsh Warehouse is the emporium of Sir Pryce-Pryce-Jones, inventor of the mail order business. You can't miss it - letters of monumental proportions are emblazoned across the top of one of the tallest buildings in the town. Railways ran special Pryce-Jones vans taking the company's goods around the country. Pryce-Jones was even patronised by Queen Victoria, not to mention my own parents who made infrequent visits from their home near Shrewsbury, as and when the furniture needed replacing.

Why do ruined churches have an air of sanctity, sometimes missing from those in use? Saint Mary's church, beside the Afon Hafren in Newtown, was abandoned many years ago due to persistent flooding and is now a well-maintained ruin, surrounded by green lawns, trees and an enclosing wall. It is a tranquil place provided with benches which on the day of my visit were largely occupied by people sitting quietly enjoying the summer sunshine.

A flamboyantly ornate Art Nouveau style railing beside the church encloses the grave and memorial of Robert Owen, champion of trade unions and co-operatives, who was born in Newtown in 1771. Tucked inside a corner of the ruined nave is something that looks like a Wendy house, but turns out to be the entrance to the Pryce-Jones vault.

The Robert Owen memorial, beside the ruins of the town's Old Saint Mary's church.

The Pryce-Jones' vault and Old Saint Mary's church.

The Kerry Hills make a striking backdrop to this lively street scene in Newtown.

139

Newtown to Bryn-y-pentre wood

From Newport the Seven Way takes a steep track through woods up into the hills, where for the first time on the route, distant Plynlimon, the source of the afon Hafren and my destination, was visible on the horizon. These hills also afford splendid views of the surrounding countryside, the Kerry ridgeway to the south being most prominent.

Rhydfelin Baptist Chapel is a deceptive building which might easily be mistaken for a small house. Lacking the expected Victorian Gothic architecture or godly texts above the entrance, it has instead boxes of well-tended geraniums fixed below plain rectangular windows. The hillside graveyard contains a sight worth seeing. Headstones, all made of the same grey Welsh slate and placed with military precision in rows, each one nearly touching its neighbour, look like the ranks of the departed on parade. The shape, ornament and letterforms vary from grave to grave but all are of a very high artistic quality.

The countryside in these hills is an agreeable mix of arable pasture and woodland. It is peaceful and unspoilt. However, Fachwen Pool for all its visual appeal, managed to convey the feeling of a municipal park. Platforms on stilts stretch out over the water from the bank at regular intervals, providing the many fishermen with easy access. Pools like these are appearing everywhere as farmers seek diversification in the face of falling incomes.

The fishermen's sport was rudely interrupted, as I looked on, by two herds of cows on opposite banks, that simultaneously decided they needed to cool off and splashed noisily into the lake, floundering around and stirring up mud.

I knew how they felt. It was a hot day and I was hot, thirsty and tired. The Severn Way does not stray far from the river valley along most of its length until it reaches Newtown, so this was the first climbing I had done for some time and it came as a shock.

A barn owl glided over the roadside hedge in the gathering dusk as I drove past the Long Myndd on my way home, the first I have seen for many years.

The afon Hafren at Caersws.

Fachwen Pool appeals to fishermen and cows alike.

140

Bryn-y-pentre wood to Caersws

Dull and overcast conditions prevailed as I walked the hills and fields between Bryn-y-pentre wood and Cearsws. Woodland glades that on a sunny day might be filled with dappled light and sunbeams looked more like the entrance to the dark forest of medieval folklore, possibly hiding in its depths goblins, giants, and red-eyed wolves, or at least a wicked witch in her hovel. Even the wildlife seemed to have gone to sleep for the day. Apart from one tree-creeper I saw little out of the ordinary.

There is not much one can say about Caersws, apart from the fact that it has two level crossings and a railway station. In fact the town has all the appearance of having grown up around the railway, in spite of the fact that the Romans had a military fort near to where the railway station now stands.

Caersws to Wigdur

A lone walker, a young woman with a heavy-looking rucksack, was approaching the only other car as I parked mine behind it at Caersws. We exchanged greetings and small talk about the Severn Way, agreeing that the only problem was that of having to walk the route twice, once to reach our daily destination and once to get back to the car. 'It's a pity we can't find someone willing to drop us off one end and pick us up the other' I suggested. 'Yes', she replied, 'but then we would have to talk to them'. A kindred spirit.

The scenery grows ever more beautiful as the surroundings become more mountainous. The mewing cries of buzzards quartering the skies are as common here as the cawing of rooks in a Worcestershire rookery.

At Gwastadcoed a small heard of bullocks, curious about my presence, edged ever closer, only to flee in panic the next moment, reappearing further on and repeating this behaviour until I climbed a stile into an enclosed track. There they were completely spooked by the sound of my camera shutter going off and stampeded to the other end of the field. I may be mistaken, but bullocks seem to be more prone to this nervous behaviour than cows.

Pegwn Mawr on the other side of the Hafren valley, a wide plateau 1,700 feet high, is now the site of a very extensive wind farm. Although regarded by many as an eye-sore, I find myself in the opposing camp. I think the silently rotating blades add drama to the horizon, rather as does, from another age, a ruined castle or the stepped silhouette of an Iron Age hill fortification. Also, from a distance, they have a playful appearance as though a bundle of children's windmills have been planted in the ground.

I have no complaints about the Severn Way exploring the hills of the upper reaches of the river, but it is a shame that the route never visits any of the alluring beaches that are visible only in the distance. Down river from Shrewsbury, where the Severn Way rarely strays from the river bank, beaches are few and far between, and then only exposed during periods of dry weather, so this characteristic of the upland river is sorely missed.

Caersws station, the busiest spot in town as a train pulls out of the station, level crossing gates open and passengers head for their parked cars.

Afon Cerist, or is it afon Trannon - the O.S. map is unclear. Whichever, it is very attractive with moorland-like banks uncluttered by trees or bushes.

Wigdwr to Llanidloes

I endured typical pressure-cooker August weather, overcast, hot and sultry. A few late roadside wild strawberries tasted good but a glass of chilled beer would have been more welcome as I trudged along the tarmac between field paths.

A female Wheatear flew from bush to bush, observing me from a safe distance but not unduly concerned. These summer visitors, called 'Whitearse' by our ancestors, had their name sanitised by the prudish Victorians. The birds old name describes its appearance perfectly, whereas 'Wheatear' is downright misleading. Its natural habitats are moors and uplands and it is rarely, if ever, seen in fields of wheat.

Much of my spare time when young was spent on mountains, moors and cliffs, where Wheatears were a common sight, but the last I saw were a pair on the Long Mynd when I was walking the Shropshire Way in April 1990. It came as a surprise that so many years had intervened.

Two features characteristic of farms in Wales and the Welsh Marches are both found at Cefn-bach. A small patch of woodland is the last resting place of generations of discarded farm machinery, household junk and a disintegrating blue van, whilst a few paces further on are two white goats tethered to old tyres. They bleated a greeting to me as I passed.

The most unexpected sight on the whole route (with the possible exception of the water buffalo at Llandrinio) is to be seen beside a house on a bend of the B4569 as it enters Allt Goch woods. A full-sized mine, of the type used for blowing up and sinking ships, floats in a pool barely large enough to contain it.

Llanidloes

Llanidloes is built near the site of an ancient ford over the afon Hafren near its confluence with the afon Clywedog. The river runs behind the town, parallel to its main street, and is particularly pleasing. Clear, shallow water, with intermittent deeper pools, flows over a bed of shale and rocks worn smooth through aeons. A footpath and small park enable the walker to follow the river along its bank for most of the length of the town centre.

Victorian, Georgian and half-timbered buildings house a variety of shops and restaurants, but the building that dominates the town is the market hall of 1600 which almost blocks the junction of the town's two main streets.

Saint Idloes' Church dates from the 7th century, though it contains an arcade of 1195-1220, believed to have been recovered from Abbey Cwmhir at the time of the Dissolution of the Monasteries. The massive 14th century tower with a two-tier timber belfry is a style commonly seen throughout the Welsh Marches. I would like to write about the hammerbeam roof and its winged angels but, as with so many churches these days, the door was locked.

In the 1830s the town's prosperity depended largely on the production of flannel. A census of the time listed six carding mills, 18 fulling mills and 35,000 spindles operating in the town and neighbourhood. Hillsides were covered in acres of finished flannel and the constant noise of looms could be heard throughout the town.

Once again the Severn Way crosses Glyndwr's Way, this time on its southern route between Knighton and Machynlleth, and for a short distance in Allt Goch woods the two routes share the same path.

The beautiful confluence of the afon Hafren and the afon Clywedog at Llanidloes.

...any of the buildings ...Llanidloes conceal ...ber-frame ...struction behind ...er frontages. A good ...mple of this is the ...phant Inn in Bridge ...reet which appears to ...built of brick but ...en viewed from the ...r yard clearly reveals ...timber-frame ...struction. However, ...National ...stminster Bank ...osite the old Market ...all, seen in the centre ...the photograph above ...t, proudly flaunts its ...26 'Arts and Crafts' ...ber-framed revival ...le.

Founded by the 7th century Saint Idloes, who gave the town its name, the church, above, stands picturesquely beside the afon Hafren and the afon Clywedog. Dendrochronology dates the timbers of the roof to 1537. Many interesting old tomb stones lean against the walls of the church.

The afon Hafren, right, rushes past a flannel mill built in 1834 beside the old bridge at the end of Short Bridge Street.

Llanidloes to Geufron

A walk of fourteen miles there and back, pushing myself, would make it possible, I hoped, to reach the source of the Hafren on Plynlimon on my next outing. As the route crossed Felindre Bridge, near Llanidloes, then turned abruptly uphill to follow the Hafren valley, I had a definite feeling that this was it. The meandering path over the hills flanking the river between Newtown and Llanidloes was behind me and ahead lay the ascent of a mountain.

I was lucky. It was a warm and sunny August day and the sky was blue with a few fleecy white clouds. The light was exceptionally good, as it often is following a period of wet weather, and there was plenty to photograph. Scrambling up a rocky watercourse I found an exposed position that gave me an unimpeded view of Hafren Forest and the head of the valley. The afon Hafren is here shrunk to a little mountain stream which is hard to reconcile with the mighty river of the Midlands and the vales of Gloucester and Berkeley.

For the first time I drove home via Llangurig, Rhayader and Knighton, rekindling memories of another walk I completed a few years back along the length of the river Wye from Chepstow to its source, which, like the Severn, is high up on Plynlimon. Indeed, the two rivers have their origins only a mile or two apart, but thereafter take very different routes before eventually becoming reunited in the Bristol Channel.

The mountains along the Upper Lye Valley looked very beautiful in the evening light, as did the northern foothills of Radnor Forest as I approached Knighton. I resolved to use that route on my next trip. If only I could find a way that avoided roadworks and traffic jams. Earlier that day, a poster for the local newspaper standing beside the road had screamed, 'Outrage at traffic delays between Bewdley and Kidderminster'. I knew. I was stuck in it. 'The kids are on holiday, their dads and mums will take them to the Safari Park. Let's dig a big hole in the middle of the road and see what happens'. It's as predictable as empty roads in November.

The magical landscape around Llanidloes is rich in folklore about fairies, witches and hauntings. Legend-tellers used to gather under an ancient horse chestnut tree on the town's Upper Green on Sundays to repeat the old stories.

Hafodfeddgar, left, and Geufron farm, right, are both situated at the top of the Hafren valley. Census returns for Geufron reveal that for 50 years, between 1841 and 1891, the farm was occupied by the same family. The size of the family, however, decreased steadily from 14 and one servant in 1841 to five and two servants in 1891, but the 1881 census shows that the land farmed had increased from 100 acres to 500 acres. The 10,000 acre Hafren forest belongs to the Forestry Commission and is the habitat of some of Britain's most attractive birds. Dippers and wagtails frequent the shallow streams, ravens haunt the mountain's rocky outcrops and, in the branches of the fir trees may be seen, if one is patient and lucky, goldcrests, siskins, and even crossbills. Mid-Wales was, for many years, the last refuge of the persecuted red kite which happily is now enjoying a recovery. This magnificent bird of prey is slightly larger than a buzzard and is easily identified in flight by its deeply-forked, chestnut-coloured tail.

Guefron to Hafren Torri Gwddf, or Severn Break-its-Neck

A narrow, winding mountain road, beginning and ending at Llanidloes, connects the Hafren and Clywedog valleys. Following the afon Hafren in the Hafren Forest, it climbs a pass before descending to the shores of the Clywedog reservoir. This is a circuit that clearly has attractions for rally drivers. As both motorist and walker I found myself repeatedly confronted by cars skidding to a halt in showers of dust and gravel, whilst others passed me at speed too close for comfort, leaving me edging perilously close to the precipice on my left.

The cars tended to come in packs. Mostly they were smallish, souped-up production models, covered in dust and dirt, driven by young men and women wearing baseball caps. A few rather larger, better-cared for, vintage models made an occasional appearance, driven by men with money. But all had one thing in common, the explosion-in-a-paint-factory look. Wavy magenta skirts on graduated yellow with ultramarine spots - that sort of thing. And, of course, a large spot on the door containing a number.

It was not one of these, but a faded blue, well-used, mud-splashed Land Rover that pulled up alongside me in the narrow road through Hafren Forest. The window wound down and leaning over, the driver asked if it was my car parked a couple of miles back in a small scooped-out recess in the hillside. Unfortunately, it was. 'I shall have to ask you to move it. We turn our tractors there', he said. At first I had difficulty believing that my car was causing an obstruction - there wasn't a farm track or gate in sight in either direction but he was insistent. The prospect of rewalking the hill I had just come up was not pleasing. 'I'll take you back and bring you hear again' he volunteered, 'or if you like you can park your car over there in front of that gate'. That sounded better, in fact it was to my advantage - my return journey would be shortened by a couple of miles. He proved to be a friendly bloke, quizzing me about the walk, proud of his local mountain scenery and dismissive of the flatlands of Gloucestershire.

Hafren Torri Gwddf, or
Severn Break-its-Neck.

hafod farm was last occupied in 1934 and can be seen near a waterfall at Blaen Hafren, together with a stone sheep dip. Hafod farms were lived in during the summer months, pasturing sheep on the surrounding hills. The census return for 1851 shows that Meredith Rees, with his wife and two daughters, a servant and two others, were living there, whilst the census for 1891 records five occupants, two of them shepherds and one, curiously, a scholar.

rom 1176 to 1536 this rea of Plynlimon rovided extensive sheep alks over 3,000 acres uring the summer onths for flocks from e nearby grange at wmbiga. The grange d the sheep belonged the monks of bbeycwmhir, 25 miles vay. The ruins of the ver's highest house, a

Hafren Torri Gwddf to the source of the river

A large rib of white calcite in the stream 200 yards below the waterfall indicates the site of Nantricket copper works where stone hammers have been found. Other evidence of mining operations can be found within the forest, notably at Nantmelin and Nant yr Eira. The former is hidden among the trees half a mile north of the nearby picnic site and was a lead mine worked first by the Romans then reworked in the 18th century.

A deep ravine at Nant yr Eira high on Plynlimon not far from the source of the afon Hafren is the site of a bronze age lead mine which also was later worked by the Romans. Archeologists have recovered bone implements from the site. Reopened in the 19th century, lead was extracted from ore transported along a tramway to a crusher powered by water from a reservoir further up the valley.

The Severn Way route up the mountain and through Hafren Forest has been much improved by a thick bed of shale and rock, quarried locally, that blends in perfectly whilst providing firm footing for the tired climber.

The sheer immensity of Hafren Forest and Plynlimon is very impressive. It has something of the grandeur and scale of the North American continent rather than the intimate landscape that we associate with Britain. From halfway up the mountain (always my favourite spot) great vistas of forested mountain ranges come into view, whilst the land beside the path has been cleared of conifers and is being colonised by a rich variety of grasses, mosses, heathers and other plants. A grey wagtail flitted ahead of me up-stream and the songs of many elusive birds came from nearby trees.

The afon Hafren drops nearly 1,500 feet between its source on Plynlimon and Llanidloes, a distance of about twelve miles. During the remaining 200 miles of the journey to the sea it falls a mere 500 feet.

At last, after a stiff climb, a stile marks the boundary of the forest and gives access to open moorland. There follows a dramatically different landscape of peat hags, bogs, sphagnum moss and endless horizons. A series of marker posts led me to the source of the river Severn, which consists of little more than two upright wooden posts beside a cotton-grass-covered bog. But that is unimportant. The source of a great river is an idea that lives in the mind and the imagination.

e Hafren, left,
fined to a narrow
untain gully.

Heather, mosses and
alpine flowers,
characteristic plants of
high mountains.

The tumbling infant
Hafren descends
Plynlimon.

Whispering wind-blown grasses and the twisted stumps of felled trees near Pumlumon Cwmbiga. Nearing this journey's destination, high on Plynlimon, the footpath passes close to Carreg Wen, a six-foot high bronze-age quartz standing stone. An inventory of 1910 records that a smaller boulder stood nearby and together they were known as 'the white cow and calf'. The people who erected this monolith were the early colonizers of these mountains. It is they who worked the mine at Nant yr Eira, and their cremated dead are buried, together with weapons, tools and pots for use in the after-life, under mounds on the bleak summit of 2,450 feet Pen Pumlumon Arwystli.

The Hafren, here little more than a ditch, is never-the-less a ditch containing crystal clear water that has yet to accumulate the sediment of the later river.

Were it not for the two upright posts identifying the source of the Hafren/Severn on Plynlimon, the exact spot could be difficult to determine. Several springs among the mossy bogs and cotton grass might claim the distinction of being the source of this great and memorable river.

John Bradford is a landscape photographer and graphic designer who, for many years, has photographed the English and Welsh countryside. The Welsh Marches and Shropshire, Herefordshire, Worcestershire and Gloucestershire are parts of the country he has extensively explored, usually on foot and invariably with a camera.

The setting sun behind a wrecked trow at Purton.

John was, for some years, a designer and art director with a design group. His interest in photography developed as he worked with professional photographers in studios and on location. Some of these projects took him to parts of Britain that he loved - the Yorkshire Moors, the English Lake District, Snowdonia and Devon among others. Returning to some of these places in his own time and with a camera he gradually developed his own skills as a photographer of landscapes. Now living in Worcestershire, only eleven miles from the Severn, this is a river he has known since his childhood in Shropshire.

His photographs have appeared in a previous book, 'Worcestershire, a portrait of the County' by Sam Redgrave, published by Halfshire Books.